Adventures of
HUCKLEBERRY
FINN

American Comic Vision

TWAYNE'S MASTERWORK STUDIES
ROBERT LECKER, GENERAL EDITOR

Adventures of
HUCKLEBERRY
FINN

American Comic Vision

David E. E. Sloane

Twayne Publishers • Boston
A Division of G. K. Hall & Co.

Adventures of Huckleberry Finn:
American Comic Vision

Twayne's Masterwork Studies No. 18

Copyright © 1988 by G. K. Hall & Co.
All rights reserved.
Published by Twayne Publishers
A division of G. K. Hall & Co.
70 Lincoln Street, Boston, Massachusetts 02111

Copyediting supervised by Barbara Sutton.
Book production by Janet Zietowski.

Typeset in 10/12 Sabon with Novarese display type
by Compset, Inc., of Beverly, Massachusetts.

Printed on permanent/durable acid-free paper
and bound in the United States of America.

Library of Congress Cataloging-in-Publication Data

Sloane, David E. E., 1943–
    Adventures of Huckleberry Finn : American comic vision / David
E. E. Sloane.
        p.   cm.—(Twayne's masterwork studies : no. 18)
    Bibliography: p.
    Includes index.
    Summary: Literary criticism of Twain's greatest work.
    ISBN 0-8057-7963-9 (alk. paper).   ISBN 0-8057-8016-5 (pbk.)
    1. Twain, Mark, 1835–1910.   Adventures of Huckleberry Finn.
2. Twain, Mark, 1835–1910—Humor.   3. Comic, The, in literature.
[1. Twain, Mark, 1835–1910.   Adventures of Huckleberry Finn.
2. American literature—History and criticism.]   I. Title.
II. Series.
PS1305.S58 1988
813'.4—dc19   88-6090
                                                                            CIP
                                                                            AC

To Lily of the Alley

Contents

Note on References and Acknowledgments

References are given by chapter in order to relate to any edition of the novel, and the Harper & Bros. facsimile with Hamlin Hill's introduction is recommended. All citations in this text to *Adventures of Huckleberry Finn* are from the Mark Twain Library edition, edited by Walter Blair and Victor Fischer (Berkeley: University of California Press, 1985). Alan Gribben's *Mark Twain's Library: A Reconstruction* (Boston:G. K. Hall, 1970) deserves mention as a valuable ready reference to check Twain's readings of other authors.

I am grateful to the Mark Twain Memorial and Elaine Cheesman and Wynn Lee for their aid, and I thank many colleagues, friends, students, and strangers who have contributed insights about Mark Twain's thinking. Robert Lucid and Bernard Duffey, should they see this work, will understand my gratitude to them for their influence as teachers and their kindness as people. Louis Budd, as always, was wonderfully helpful and kind in his thoughtful advice.

I would like to acknowledge the help of my wife, Bonnie Fausz Sloane, during the composition of this book. I also want to thank University of New Haven Dean Joseph Chepaitis, Provost Alex Sommers, and President Phillip Kaplan for released time to work on a first draft of this book.

Mark Twain (Samuel Clemens), ca. 1881–85.
Courtesy of Mark Twain Memorial, Hartford, CT.

Chronology:
Mark Twain's Life and Works

1835	Samuel Langhorne Clemens, the sixth of seven children, born in Florida, Missouri, on 30 November to Jane Lampton Clemens and John Marshall Clemens.
1839	Failing as a storekeeper, Clemens moves his family to Hannibal, Missouri, and engages in business; he practices at various times as justice of the peace, attorney, and president of the Library Association.
1847	Judge Clemens dies. Sam Clemens begins working as an apprentice printer.
1852	On 1 May *The* (Boston) *Carpet-Bag* publishes "The Dandy Frightening the Squatter"; the (Philadelphia) *American Courier* publishes a sketch of Hannibal, by "S.L.C." one week later. The two pieces are the young writer's first appearance in eastern periodicals.
1853–1857	Travels as a journeyman printer and corresponds with his brother Orion's Muscatine (Iowa) *Journal*; works as a printer for Orion in Keokuk, Iowa, before leaving for Cincinnati.
1857	In April, apprentices to learn piloting on the Mississippi River.
1861	In July, as the Civil War breaks out, accompanies Orion to Nevada.
1862–1864	Reports for the Virginia City (Nevada) *Territorial Enterprise*. "Mark Twain" appears in February 1863.
1864	Artemus Ward meets reporter Mark Twain, drinks with him, and lectures in his presence, later encouraging Twain to come east with him because Twain is wasting himself among the sagebrush.
1864	Reports for the San Francisco *Call*, but leaves town, frustrated by the *Call*'s restraint, and difficulties deriving from his political and business satires.

1865   "The Celebrated Jumping Frog of Calaveras County" appears in Henry Clapp's New York *Saturday Press* on 18 November to instant popular success, gaining Twain national recognition as a western humorist.

1866   From January through March, visits Hawaii as correspondent for the Sacramento *Union*; he gives first public lecture, on the Sandwich Islands (Hawaii), in San Francisco on 2 October.

1867   C. H. Webb publishes the "Celebrated Jumping Frog" and other stories as a book in New York. Twain embarks on the *Quaker City*, a steamboat bound for Europe and the Holy Land under the auspices of Henry Ward Beecher's Plymouth Church. As reporter for the San Francisco *Alta California*, continues a series of travel letters written from the viewpoint of a western American vandal; on his return he will begin lecturing on "the vandal abroad."

1869   *Innocents Abroad* published by the American Publishing Company of Hartford, Connecticut. William Dean Howells's review initiates one of Twain's most important literary friendships. Twain buys one-third interest in the Buffalo (New York) *Express*, but soon tires of newspaper editing. Begins an active lecturing career.

1870   Marries Olivia Langdon, daughter of a wealthy coal dealer, in Elmira, New York, on 2 February. Their bliss is soon disrupted by the death of Livy's father, her nervous collapse, and the premature birth of son Langdon Clemens.

1871   The family moves to Nook Farm in Hartford, Connecticut.

1872   Susan is born in March, but Langdon dies in June; Twain visits England during the later part of the year to universal acclaim. *Roughing It* published.

1873   Twain and Charles Dudley Warner's collaborative novel *The Gilded Age* published.

1874   Clara is born, the only member of Twain's immediate family to outlive him. Howells publishes "A True Story" in the November *Atlantic Monthly*, helping to secure Twain's claim as a serious humor writer.

1875   "Old Times on the Mississippi," published serially in the *Atlantic Monthly*, identifies Twain with the Southwest and the Mississippi River as well as the West.

1876   *The Adventures of Tom Sawyer* published. A sequel, using Tom's sidekick Huck Finn as narrator, is begun but stalls about chapter 16 and is laid aside for Twain's "tank," as he calls his inspiration, to refill.

Chronology

1877	Is embarrassed when Boston Brahmins fail to be amused by his speech describing three tramps impersonating Holmes, Emerson, and Longfellow, delivered at John G. Whittier's birthday dinner on 17 December.
1878–1879	Family travels in Europe.
1880	Jean, the last of Twain's children, born in July. *A Tramp Abroad,* a burlesque walking tour of Europe including some of Twain's best western sketches, is published.
1882	*The Prince and the Pauper* published to the applause of Nook Farm and the distress of Westerners, who feel Twain has lost his true vein.
1883	*Life on the Mississippi* published as a book, expanding "Old Times on the Mississippi" from the *Atlantic* and including a long excerpt about a boy among flatboatmen borrowed from the narrative of Huck Finn, which Twain claims to have been working on in a desultory way for the past five or six years and expects to finish in five or six more.
1884–1885	Lectures with G. W. Cable, revisits the Mississippi, and publishes excerpts from *Huckleberry Finn* in the December 1884 *Century Magazine;* later installments appear in January and February 1885 to some controversy. *Adventures of Huckleberry Finn* published in Britain in 1884 to secure British copyright; published in 1885 by the Charles L. Webster Co. of New York.
1888	Yale awards Mark Twain an honorary A. M. degree.
1889	*A Connecticut Yankee in King Arthur's Court* published, seriously damaging Twain's British book sales because of its irreverence toward things British. Franklin D. Roosevelt later describes his programs by using Hank Morgan's phrase "New Deal."
1891–1895	Twain and family reside in Europe.
1894	*Pudd'nhead Wilson* published, in which Roxy's one-sixteenth black blood "outvotes" the rest to make her a slave. Twain is bankrupted in April by the Paige typesetter.
1895	In August, begins around-the-world lecture tour to pay off debts incurred when the Paige typesetter forces him into bankruptcy.
1896	Susie Clemens dies; *Joan of Arc* published.
1897	*Following the Equator* published.
1904	Livy dies in Florence, Italy, after years of intermittent illness.

1906	*What Is Man?*, pessimistic determinism by Twain, privately published.
1907	Oxford University awards Twain a Litt.D. degree.
1908	Twain moves to Stormfield, in Redding, Conn.
1909	Jean dies in December.
1910	Mark Twain dies 21 April 1910 at Redding, Connecticut, to international mourning. William Dean Howells publishes *My Mark Twain*, calling Clemens "sole, incomparable, the Lincoln of our literature."

— 1 —

Historical Context

Visiting Hartford, Connecticut, in 1869, Mark Twain mused that he never was in a city where huckleberries and morality grew so profusely. Representatively southwestern and skeptical, the remark highlights the sensitivity of a frontier humorist who had already won a reputation as the "Moralist of the Main." Like other midwestern Americans—Abraham Lincoln, John Hay, William Dean Howells, Thomas Alva Edison—Twain was the product of the small-town experience that expressed democratic philosophy more egregiously than Washington, Jefferson, and Hamilton could ever have imagined. Uproarious voters had ground pieces of a giant cheese into the White House rugs as it dripped from their bowie knives while celebrating Andrew Jackson's election in 1828. Since then, the practical man had found his own expectations mirrored in the educational, geographical, and mechanical improvements of the nation as Horace Mann convinced northerners of the importance of education; as Polk and Harrison presided over the filling out of the nation's natural boundaries; and as Eli Whitney demonstrated interchangeability of parts as the basic technique of mass manufacture.

The Civil War brought a deeper awareness of moral issues through the problem of the Negro slave. The universal Yankee nation agreed on the importance of the republic, but only a segment of the North was committed to abolition. Southerners satirized northerners as mudsills: "spirits careless whom they annoy, and utterly indifferent to all things, unless . . . treasured up carefully from boyhood, in the leaves of Poor Richard," Benjamin Franklin's Quaker moralist.[1] To northerners a degree of vulgarity blended into the rise of the middle class, as aptly portrayed in Howells's *The Rise of Silas Lapham* (1885) and Henry James's *The American* (1877). Twain himself was declared unacceptable in a number of northern drawing rooms; the wife of Thomas Bailey Aldrich refused to invite him to dinner because he appeared drunk, so odd seemed his mannerisms. The preoccupation with moral purpose in bluestocking New England seemed equally odd to the westerner Twain, despite his own intense moral concerns as a philosopher-humorist.

The twin peaks of nineteenth-century American life were the Constitution and the King James Bible. Literary comedians like Artemus Ward would wryly comment that the world turned on its axis in obedience to the former document, subject only to money-getting as a national pastime. P. T. Barnum's entrepreneurial patriotism stimulated Ward to pose as an "Old Showman" who presented moral drama and platform lectures criticizing the crowned heads of Europe and "Seceshers," and pioneering the role of vandal abroad—Twain used this last persona as a vehicle to rise to fame in 1869. The failure of Radical Reconstruction left many northerners bitter, as suggested by the titles of novels on the subject such as Albion Tourgee's *A Fool's Errand* (1879) written "by one of the fools," and *Bricks Without Straw* (1880), which criticized the failure to enfranchise the black American truly and rectify the original wrongs of the Constitution.

The *Century* magazine and *Lippincott's* in the 1870s and 1880s attempted to bind the nation's Civil War wounds by celebrating the American regions in all their literary local color. Rollin Osterweis, in *The Myth of The Lost Cause, 1865–1900,* shows their attempts at healing the wounds, however, as coinciding with a conscious southern strategy to win by social control what they had lost in the North's "War of Aggression," as the South saw the "War of Secession."[2] So the great magazines bordered on neutrality, chronicling the Civil War through such exhaustive studies as Nicolay and Hay's ten-volume life of Lincoln, but also granting space in their pages for accounts written by former rebels. Twain's liberalism had grown increasingly profound as the issue of Negro slavery focused for him all the issues of moral, intellectual, and emotional slavery in his own personality. Aware of the resurgence of anti-black sentiment, as Shelly Fisher Fishkin suggests he was in 1876, Mark Twain undertook to write his greatest book. He may have stalled as much from a resurgence of racism in 1876 in the newspapers of the day as from the drift of Huck's raft past Cairo, Illinois, in what is now chapter 16 of the novel, making it impossible for Huck and Jim to canoe up the Ohio River and escape slave-hunting parties crossing into Illinois from the Missouri side of the Mississippi River. The Civil Rights Bill of 1866, as amended by Charles Sumner to protect Negro rights to public conveyance, service, and education was defeated in 1872, again in 1874, and only passed in 1875, to be declared unconstitutional in the states by the Supreme Court in 1883, remaining operable only in Washington, D.C., and the territories. The irony of black people's civil rights in the democracy was ongoing. As the final draft of *Huck Finn* was being written, the status of blacks continued to be an issue of national importance.[3]

In 1876, as the nation celebrated its centennial, the United States was about to enter into a new era of growth as a world power. By the 1880s, questions about the manipulation of that power by plutocrats and politicians were already becoming a troubling counterpoint to the theme of never-ending progress, the antidote to superstition, ignorance, and poverty offered by the New World to the Old. The forces of literary realism were thrusting ever less palatable scenes, subjects, and characters into the cultural life of the well-to-do. The corruption of the Grant Regime demonstrated even to Grant's supporters that democracy could harbor as much badness as did monarchy. A radical expansion of the middle and upper middle classes raised new questions of manners. Twain's own drift from West to East and from newsroom to drawing room was representative of American upward mobility, with its attendant personal and spiritual issues, in particular the unique insecurity that characterized the modern democracy. The emotional and spiritual questions of this era, added to the patriotic instincts and ethical concerns of the pre–Civil War midwestern American, now risen to the level of national and international spokesman, became the elements Mark Twain fused into *Adventures of Huckleberry Finn*.

– 2 –

The Importance of the Work

Few books have been so seriously or so often nominated for the Great American Novel as *Adventures of Huckleberry Finn*. Few authors have remained so steadily in the limelight as important cultural-historical figures as Mark Twain, whose sponsorship of a black student at Yale was front-page news as recently as 1985.[4] So complex is the central issue of *Huck Finn*, the acceptance by Huck of his responsibility to Jim, a "nigger," that argument over the book's racism continues. No comparable major novel has been so persistently the target of censors of manners, morals, or misguided racial consciousness. From 1885 to the present moment, *Huck Finn* has been banned from the shelves of libraries and schools throughout the nation more often than any other "classic" work in the American literary canon.

Adventures of Huckleberry Finn describes how a white boy, with a "sound heart but a deformed conscience," in Twain's words, overcomes his southern background and training and helps a runaway Negro slave escape to freedom. Chronicling their trip down the Mississippi, the plot uses American frontier materials to grapple with central American issues of freedom, equality, humanity, and conscience. Twain shows corruption as it appears in America's small towns and the frauds who prey on it; his novel indicts society for its pointless feuds, its false religion, and its misplaced sense of social prestige and honor; a host of related ideas in the book center on tawdry culture and unconscious cruelty. The image of the raft on the Mississippi

River, however, offers a positive alternative where Huck and Jim develop a finer relationship—a sensibility, couched in natural imagery and personal understanding, which raises the book to the level of visionary literature and gives it its lasting worldwide importance as an expression of American democratic impulses.

Huck's language and pose show the elevation of natural American materials to the level of high art. Ernest Hemingway, H. L. Mencken, William Dean Howells, Joel Chandler Harris, D. H. Lawrence, and Edgar Lee Masters, among other important authors, have found the texture of *Huck Finn* arresting. Huck's language and personality as first-person narrator forms the medium of the novel. He expresses concepts in deadpan irony close to Mark Twain's platform pose. He depicts scenes in unique images and diction using vulgarly descriptive words and colloquialisms never previously used in idealistic literature. He describes plot events and action in clipped restrained sentences, free from the didactic moralizations typical of books aimed at the young in the nineteenth century. If all American literature comes from *Huck Finn*, as Hemingway claimed, the special language of Huck and the ideology that it cloaks expresses the persona of Mark Twain lying just under the surface of the fictional character Huck Finn, and, ultimately, the vision of Samuel Langhorne Clemens. The language pretends to be an accurate reflection of frontier vernacular, and Twain's dialectal accuracy has often been praised, but the language is actually a much more sophisticated tool. It raises the novel beyond literary realism to a plane of natural idealism which combines and embodies the higher forms of romanticism and realism in literary humor.

Attempts to ban *Adventures of Huckleberry Finn* as racist, in Chicago and other communities, continue because of its use of the word "nigger," 206 times by one count. The book's estimate of men, not merely blacks but all Americans, however, represents an important American identity. With over 150 editions in print, selling over a quarter of a million copies a year, if American sales are added to the panoply of foreign translations in German, French, Russian and other major world languages, *Huckleberry Finn* is one of the most steadily experienced projections of America and the American spirit. The image of the raft and the river provides an appropriate cultural symbol for a nation that sees itself as continuously changing. The go-getter spirit, admired in the universal Yankee nation from its founding, is wedded to an intuitive moral idealism that overwhelms social dictates. Huck represents the finer motive in the democratic tradition.

The importance of *Huckleberry Finn* is thus twofold. First, Huck

Finn, its narrator, espouses an ethic of egalitarian—that is, demo-cratic—concern with his fellow man which makes him the quintessen-tial American, taking all men as equals, accepting all men according to their humanity. He accords all men equal rights under God. Second, his language and his mental and emotional nature express his univer-sal kindliness in first-person uninterrupted colloquialism. Twain's freeing of such native materials from restraint leads directly to modern American fiction, but, at the same time, the realism of Twain's por-trayal caused, and still causes, many critics to reject parts of the book and parts of Huck's thinking. Finally, the ethic of "right and kind"—the raft ethic—gives a universal interpretation to the egalitarian ideal, and raises the novel to the level of vision.

— 3 —

Critical Reception

From before its first publication, *Adventures of Huckleberry Finn* was the object of contention. A whole chapter describing flatboatmen was dropped when Twain's publisher and nephew, Charles Webster, wanted to reduce the size of the book, and a number of words were altered by readers of the manuscript. The question of the actual impact of editorial changes suggested by William Dean Howells and Livy Langdon Clemens remains moot. From Van Wyck Brooks through the present, many critics have complained that the authentic Mark Twain of the frontier was weakened and compromised by emending harshly realistic diction to comic euphemisms in Huck's language. Bernard DeVoto in *Mark Twain at Work* (1942) comments on such changes as Huck's description of Pap Finn from "drunk" to "mellow" as softenings, a complaint echoed as recently as 1987. However, such presumed concessions to Victorian gentility may represent the hand of the humorist modifying sterner realism more akin to the naturalism of the 1890s into comedy, a wholly different transaction than his giving up the sternness of his central message. Clemens's acceptance of editing of tone may be part of his strength as an author rather than a loss of crucial roughness.

Before publication, excerpts of *Huck Finn* appeared in the pages of Richard Watson Gilder's restrainedly adventurous *Century* magazine, which had just finished serializing John Hay's controversial

Bread-Winners, in which the hero dallies with and even kisses a poor girl in a suggestive and seductive way. Hay's work drew outraged protests from readers. The portions of *Huck Finn* that Gilder's *Century* published in the December 1884 and the January and February 1885 issues included some of *Huck Finn's* racier material: the Grangerford-Shepherdson Feud and the raft idyl; Jim and Huck's "Was Sollermun Wise?" discussion; the Royal Nonesuch episode where the king cavorts around in painted stripes and no clothes, a variation on an old frontier gag; the Camp Meeting scene, with young girls kissing the fraudulent king; the killing of old Boggs in cold blood by Col. Sherburn; and the Wilks episodes. But in the magazine the description of Bricksville's main street—with its ugly picture of loafers dousing dogs with kerosene and torching them—was deleted, and all references to nudity either on the raft or in the Royal Nonesuch disappeared; kissing at the camp meeting and the details of Peter Wilks's corpse vanish, as does the Duke's cynicism about obscenity, "There, if that line don't fetch them, I don't know Arkansaw!" Even with all these deletions, however, as Arthur Scott has recorded, Gilder still had to defend the book against angry school superintendents, allowing that Clemens was "at times . . . inartistically and indefensibly coarse."

Twain's wife, Livy, and William Dean Howells suggested various deletions of Twain's more vulgarly realistic slang. Yet, Clara Clemens in *My Father Mark Twain* quotes Howells, on 14 November 1884, as commenting on a Twain performance, "I thought the bits from Huck Finn told the best—at least I enjoyed them most. That is a mighty good book, and I should like to hear you read it all."[5] T. S. Perry's "Mark Twain," published in the *Century* in May 1885, labelled Huck an "immortal hero." Perry noted the strengths of various episodes, and was firm in his enthusiasm for *Huck Finn* as superior to *Tom Sawyer.*

More painful than Clemens cared to admit, perhaps, was the attack on *Huck Finn* by the Concord Library Committee of Concord, Massachusetts. Despite Twain's humorous references to having created his own moral scaffolding since the 1870s, an understanding acceptance of his "sermons" still meant much to him. The committee attacked the book as "coarse" and "dealing with a series of experiences not elevating . . . being more suited to the slums than to intelligent, respectable people."[6]

The other shot heard round Boston's influential critical world noted in *The Critic* of 6 June 1885 was that the book was "irreligious." But even here counterclaims suggested that the book could be and was used as a moral instructor in the prison library of the New York State Reformatory. Arthur Vogelback in his study of the book's reception even found the *Arkansaw Traveler* castigating obscenity and vulgarity—the Arkansas hostility was a victim's response to being fetched by the Royal Nonesuch and lampooned for lack of culture in the "ladies and children not admitted" remark. Twain's response to his publisher was a chortle of glee at the "puff" from Concord and a mock preface in which he suggested that Huck was the boy-portrait of the editors in Boston and Springfield who attacked him, only in Huck he had shown their language "toned down and softened." *The Critic* (edited by the Gilders) of 5 March 1885 printed the *Springfield Republican*'s hostile notice in equal type with an adulatory statement from the *Saturday Review,* dramatizing the sharp differences on the book's value as humor and as moral fiction: realistic, wild, and tender, all at once, in the more favorable view.

The critical reception of the book was broad, even though the more formal literary magazines of the period seldom reviewed "popular" books. In Britain, *The Literary World* of 16 January 1885 praised "genuine laughter-raising wit, a little coarse sometimes, but never downright vulgar," as if vulgarity were possible with Livy, Howells, Webster, and Twain himself all determined to sanitize the text appropriately. The *World* also said, "an immeasurable distance separates him from his would-be rivals" among other American humorists, quoting the crucial first four passages of the novel and Jim's view of Sollermun. The *Congregationalist* of March 1885 found "abundant material for serious thought", and the *British Quarterly Review* of January 1885 saw Twain, "a little coarse, sometimes a little irreverent" but "with a prevailing dryness and sense of reality which do much to compensate for offences against taste." Recognizing that the book was above pedestrian criticisms, the editorial writer of London's *Saturday Review* of 2 April 1887 responded tartly to a notice of Twain as second only to Artemus Ward and Bret Harte: "This is the short view of the author of *Huckleberry Finn.*"

Two comments on the book from 1885 bear special note, those by Brander Matthews and Joel Chandler Harris, both writers and significant advocates of literary realism and local color. Idealists and romantics alike were growing increasingly hostile to the realism of the vulgar and commonplace because it degraded life through repulsive details; it limited fantasy and escape to higher planes. Harris digressed on the occasion of Twain's semicentennial as celebrated by *The Critic* on 28 November 1885 to give *Huckleberry Finn* a ringing endorsement: "His last book is better than his first, and there his youth is renewed and revived. I know that some of the professional critics will not agree with me, but there is not in our fictive literature a more wholesome book than 'Huckleberry Finn.' It is history, it is romance, it is life. Here we behold human character stripped of all tiresome details; we see people growing and living; we laugh at their humor, share their griefs; and, in the midst of it all, behold we are taught the lesson of honesty, justice and mercy" (7:253). The essential moral quality of Twain's novel was thus raised in direct contradiction to the salvos from Massachusetts. Later scholars have undervalued the magnitude of this response as a defence of both realism and ethical force in Twain's writing. In 1905, in a congratulatory letter to the Mark Twain seventieth birthday dinner, Harris would go on to call *Huck Finn* the Great American Novel. Brander Matthews in the *Saturday Review* of 31 January 1885 not only praised Twain's realism but claimed that he raised "the photograph to the region of art." Matthews noted that "Old maids of either sex will wholly fail to understand him or to like him, or to see his significance and his value." He particularly praised the depiction of Huck from the inside not the outside, without speeches put in his mouth, and he praised Jim as ranking with the other great recent portraits of the Negro. So firmly was Matthews committed to his viewpoint that he included the essay in his slim volume of essays, *Americanisms and Briticisms* (1892), under the title "Mark Twain's Best Story."

By the turn of the century, *Huckleberry Finn* and Twain had become American icons, and in cartoons Twain was as often shown with a fishing rod and straw hat as behind a pilot wheel.[7] Although Edgar Lee Masters rated *Tom Sawyer* above *Huck Finn,* H. L. Mencken described reading it as a major event in his life. James T. Farrell, Ernest Hemingway, and others treated it with respect. Masters theorized that Twain had sold out to the Reverend Joe Twichell's "Church of the Holy Speculators"; *Huck Finn* ran riot with the entry of the Duke and Dauphin and failed to criticize American society through the two frauds. He complained that Huck's dialect was inconsistent and often literary, as indeed it is. He pointed out Twain's real method in Pap Finn's "Call this a govment" speech: "It is close enough to reality to sustain the humor, and far enough from reality to make one see that it is really satire on situations and characters more real and credible."[8] However, Masters concluded that this speech did not scathe the shoddy and putrid government of the day as it should have.

Critical Reception

The ultimate ironic reversal came with Van Wyck Brooks in *The Ordeal Of Mark Twain* (New York: Dutton, 1920). Brooks, with the love of controversy and blindness to external history that make literary criticism and psychological analysis truly fascinating enterprises, attacked not *Huck Finn*'s coarseness but its concessions to Victorian prudishness, Twain's willing self-suppression in the quest for acceptance and success among the genteel. Bernard DeVoto in *Mark Twain's America* (1932) fired back from the Mississippi heartland that the book followed a truly American wandering down the river of the American spirit. Lionel Trilling's "Introduction to *Huckleberry Finn*" (New York: Rinehart, 1948), often reprinted, recognizes the river as a "great brown god," the conveyer of Twain's immediacy of language, flexibility, and moral truth; his essay remains one of the finest examples of graceful and perceptive literary analysis in modern criticism. In *Mark Twain At Work* DeVoto drifted closer to Brooks in noting the editing of the manuscript, tilting the final text toward Twain's Victorian readers, and Brooks likewise drifted over the years closer to DeVoto.

By the 1950s, academic critics began to discuss the special nature of the vernacular voice of Huck, the novel's structure, the psychology of its hero, imagery, and folk motifs; discussion of the novel as a picaresque adventure remained an ongoing concern as did the problem with the last fifth of the book where the action diminishes first because the events are under Tom Sawyer's control and second because Twain developed an elaborate burlesque of romance fiction. The reemergence of Tom Sawyer to dominate the last fifth of the novel continues to be the largest critical "problem." Barry A. Marks's *Mark Twain's Huckleberry Finn* (Boston: Heath, 1959) provides one of the finest collections of essays to show the debates between proponents of *Huck Finn* as the Great American Novel and those seeing it as a badly flawed classic, including seminal essays by Trilling, Brooks, DeVoto, Marx, Cox, O'Connor and others; it is an excellent reflection of the best thinking on the novel from 1910 through 1960.

From the 1960s on, criticism has expanded in almost every specialized direction. The best treatment of the novel from a psychological viewpoint remains Jose Barchilon and J. S. Kovel's "*Huckleberry Finn*: A Psychoanalytic Study." (Journal of the American Psychoanalytic Association [1966]). Critics of the 1970s and 1980s have added to their analyses an element of deconstruction that traces the progress of the novel back to psychosocial forces buried beneath the surface of the narrative. The focus of contemporary criticism remains with the details of the literary construction of pieces of the novel and on the failure of the last fifth of the novel to allow Huck and Jim a true bonding and escape from the shore world. The most recent collections of essays devoted to *Adventures of Huckleberry Finn* include an issue of the magazine *Proteus* (Fall 1984) and a centennial collection of twenty-four essays titled *One Hundred Years of Huckleberry Finn,* published by the University of Missouri Press in 1985.

The final irony of the book's reception by the critics is not its ongoing expulsion from high school libraries. A range of black politicians and educators now attack the book for its "anti-Negro" position. A symposium appears as "Black Writers on *Adventures of Huckleberry Finn* One Hundred Years Later," *Mark Twain Journal* (Fall 1984), in which nine essays probe this question; Leslie Fiedler in "*Huckleberry Finn*: The Book We Love to Hate" also confronts it in the 1984 *Proteus* symposium. Editions of *Huck Finn* have appeared with the roughly 200 uses of "nigger" removed or sanitized but even the now-restored illustrations by E. W. Kemble lean on the comic Negro stereotype; Kemble later published *Kemble's Coons,* subtitled "A Collection of Southern Sketches" (New York: Russell, 1896), which followed the stock Negro portraits. Unquestionably, Huck's response to "Was anybody hurt?"—"No'm, killed a nigger"—needs thoughtful and sympathetic interpretation to a young black reader. The word "nigger" is one of the most uncompromising parts of Twain's realism, and an understandably upsetting one for a black youth to assimilate. Twain showed the level of respect he saw in America, and so the treatment of Jim by society retains an appropriate consistency with the rest of the novel.

Now that the centennial observance of *Huck Finn*'s publication has passed, surveys of the last fifty and hundred years of criticism offer valuable historical insights in addition to their literary analysis. Hamlin Hill's introduction to the Harper & Row facsimile edition (1987) is one, Louis Budd's "The Recomposition of *Adventures of Huckleberry Finn,*" (*Missouri Review,* 10:1 [1987]), another, and John C. Gerber's introduction to *One Hundred Years of Huckleberry Finn* (Columbia: University of Missouri Press, 1985), another. The paperback California edition of *Adventures of Huckleberry Finn* (1985) carries substantial scholarly apparatus documenting sources of characters and places in the novel, as well as notable editorial points. With full scholarly apparatus from the University of California Press in hardbound edition to be published later, both editions claim to represent a text more accurate than even Twain achieved in the first edition. The critical reception, now dignified by the massive Iowa-California edition of Twain's canon, validates Mark Twain as one of our truly great figures and *Adventures of Huckleberry Finn,* as never before, a central artifact of American culture.

A Reading

– 4 –

Undermining Authority

In 1885 the Concord Library Board pulled *Huck Finn* from its shelves. What could possibly have been so offensive in this humorous book, seemingly directed at children, planned for door-to-door sales by a popular writer? Modern sensibilities are certainly affronted by the author's frequent use of the racist epithet "nigger," and the Concord Library Board was angered by the low tone generally. Is the treatment of the Negro, most easily addressed as a surface issue in the word "nigger," so callous, so racist, and so racially insensitive that the Concordians were right? Is there more in the book that was offensive, contrary to acceptable norms, hostile to important values? Or was the book, as Robert Bridges, the critic for *Life* (26 February 1885), contended, merely "blood curdling" trash, battening on murder and melodrama? Concord's dissatisfaction with *Adventures of Huckleberry Finn* keeps abstract critical apparatus in perspective. If the book is the Great American Novel, or at least a contender for the title, these points must be debated and a higher ethic found in its pages. The book is filled with challenging social portraits and actions by low characters; it often shows degraded and uncivilized behavior, frequently with the approval of the narrator-hero Huckleberry Finn. Our critical analysis must contribute to an understanding of these problems. Was the Concord Library Board right? If not, why not? Or, is the novel, indeed, the Great American Novel, raising American scenes and American ideals to their finest fictional expression?

A great work of literature combines art and ideology. The reader's response to the author's philosophy is thereby elevated to the highest possible level of intensity. Since *Huck Finn* is under discussion as the Great *American* Novel, furthermore, its ideology should be in some way American and democratic in spirit, consistent with Twain's background and his other writings. The book should offer a compelling story, enhanced by the kinds of literary techniques that heighten a reader's pleasure, identification with the hero and emotional response. Consequently, we need two discussions, one concerning the book's social message and the other concerning its quality as a novel. Since I have decided to call *Adventures of Huckleberry Finn* the Great American Novel, I will contend that it is outstanding on both points.

Kenneth Burke, in "Psychology and Form" and "Lexicon Rhetoricae," two brief essays in his book *Counterstatement* (Berkeley: University of California Press, 1968), writes that the most profound effects of a work of art are created by the repetition of form; the creation of expectations in a reader through repeated and carefully varied devices, as well as through information, enhances our excitement about information by baffling our emotional expectation, and finally satisfies us with increasingly complex style and devices as well as with plot complications. Language, symbolism, and dramatic action fuse at the end of the work. Burke cautions us to beware of the tyranny of the informational, as characters, and even authors—especially the humorist Twain—frequently offer false information; they lie for effect. Burke's method has much to offer students of *Adventures of Huckleberry Finn*. Twain's melodrama battens on the symphonic interaction between the overall form of the novel in plot, characters, setting, and minor forms of elaboration: word choice, repetition, allusion, simile, and metaphor. Lionel Trilling was right to emphasize the great Mississippi River as the god of the novel, for within that medium a wealth of divergent materials are drawn to their climax, but the smaller elements in themselves often repeat, develop, alter, or first frustrate and then release the energy of readers' responses to Huck's raft-voyage. If all levels of the novel enhance its major themes and expand the emotional response of the reader, then the book is indeed a masterwork: our answer to the Concord Library Board.

Second, the study of the text of an American novel is not ever really complete in and of itself. American ideology is too pervasive in our culture, and Twain's environment as an author offers special insights into both historical and modern readings of the novel. Twain's awareness of American society, of his own morals and ethics, and of his position as an American humorous writer add dimensions to *Adventures of Huckleberry Finn*. The book began as a sequel to *The Adventures of Tom Sawyer*, which tapped into the nostalgia of Americans both for childhood and the village life thought to have disappeared with the Civil War. It addressed a popular audience more politically conscious than audiences in other nations. It borrowed freely from the American comic tradition. Twain's reputation as a regional writer of the South and West determined his choice of scene, but his life in Hartford, Connecticut, enhanced crucial components of his personality. Consequently, insights can be gained by comparing points in the novel to other contemporary novels such as John T. Trowbridge's to discover how Twain managed his work as a work of philosophy and a work of art. Trowbridge (1827–1916) was a popular humorous writer of the Civil War and post–Civil War period first known for his antislavery novel *Neighbor Jackwood* (1857). He produced a number of children's novels, but he also wrote *A Picture of the Desolated States* (1868), a long travel narrative of a visit to the slave states after the Civil War that emphasized humorous anecdotes; *Cudjo's Cave* (1864),a melodramatic war novel dealing with the moral issues and attendant adventures surrounding slavery, brutality, and freedom in 1861; and "Young Joe," a short story featuring a rough boy hunter who educates a city-bred adult in woodcraft, published in *Young Joe and Other Boys* (1879). Thus, Trowbridge provides comparisons between Twain and a contemporary writer using similar materials concerned with the issues of the Civil War and post–Civil War period. In fact, Twain, meeting him in June 1908, told Trowbridge he had listened to his stories while he was being rocked in the cradle, according to A. B. Paine's biography of Twain.

My analysis will proceed more or less directly through the novel, but the emphasis will follow the major moments of the book. First, while discussing the introductory chapters through about chapter 16, I will focus on elements that free Huck from authority: Huck's conflicts with Miss Watson, the widow Douglas, and Pap. Although some of Twain's finest dialect effects occur later, dialect is an important consideration. In a great work we expect the major themes to be announced early, and so they are here. Twain foreshadows his climactic moments from the first page of the novel. Second, in discussing the adventures while Huck and Jim raft down the Mississippi, I will focus on the book as a social statement leading to one of the great climactic moments in American literature, Huck's decision to go to hell for Jim's sake, a moment whose power is enhanced by his earlier scepticism toward Miss Watson's view of Providence. Each of the raft episodes elaborates Twain's view of society as filtered through Huck's sensibility and spoken in Huck's voice. Finally, the climax of the novel and the last fifth of the book, when Huck and Jim are subordinated to Tom Sawyer's games, takes on increased significance when addressed in Burkean terms as a symphonic elaboration of the first three chapters of the book, now modified subtly by the raft experience. These chapters, while less compelling than the raft journey to many readers and critics, are appropriate, and in fact darkly meaningful, for our understanding of the novel as an American classic.

Even the cover of the first edition made clear to its audience that *Adventures of Huckleberry Finn* was a "folksy" book, ornamented for the subscription trade where salesmen sold books door-to-door. Vines and crossed driftwood boards for the capital letters *H* and *F* set off a picture of Huck. The frontispiece shows Huck Finn, a boy of about fourteen, holding a long rifle in one hand and in the other a dead jackrabbit hanging by the legs. Huck's straw hat has a bite taken out of it; his baggy pants are held up too high by their single suspender. E. W. Kemble's name is prominent as the artist in the bottom left corner of the cartoon, with the date 1884. Facing Kemble's cartoon of Huck is a formal photograph of a marble bust of Mark Twain, underscored by the scrawled "Mark Twain" signature. Thus, the novel actually offered some rather imposing elements within its humorous format. The informal full-figure portrait of Huck grants him a raffish presence and mischievous identity before the book begins. Twain's bust facing the full-length Huck portrait is also notable. Louis Budd has suggested that Twain added the formal bust to suggest a seriousness in his work, and the prominence of Kemble's name on his engraving also suggests a willingness to be identified with the book. *Adventures of Huckleberry Finn* is thus buttressed by the trappings of a serious book even more fully than *The Prince and the Pauper* which had been introduced by serious visual artifacts in 1882: a reproduction of a historical document and the picture of two sides of an archaic English coin. Like the earlier book, *Adventures of Huckleberry Finn* had pretensions to "serious humor."

Twain's "Notice" to the reader carries out this manipulation of mood. He claims he will prosecute "motive" seekers, banish "moral" seekers, and shoot plot-lovers. His suggestion that persons attempting to find a plot will be shot fits well with his entire canon—Twain's best books were plotless picaresque narratives in which he could immerse his hero in fast-paced comic and tragic scenes as a dead-pan ironic observer. If we accept E. M. Forster's definition of a plot, in *Aspects of the Novel* (1927), as a series of events connected by causation, however, Twain's disclaimer is obviously an act of comic indirection, for events in *Huck Finn* are connected by several compelling causes as the action extends: Huck's determination not to return to Pap, the widow, and St. Petersburg, and his larger determination to help Jim escape on the raft. Twain's reference to motives and morals is an even more loaded act of comic indirection. Presumably, the reader of a boy's humor book would not be looking for a moral. Twain's denial is too much of a protest; it may be, if the reader had not already suspected *Huck Finn* to be a serious book, that Twain's Notice was intended to put the idea of morality in the reader's mind, and it does so. The humorist works in reverse, with a warning by the Chief of Ordnance—that is, the "big gun"—an easy suggestion that someone important had identified the motivation of the book and wished to deny it. In miniature, Twain's warning provides a deadpan foreshadowing of the development of the novel's action, as Huck first denies and then later backs into his moral actions. An "Explanatory" then goes on to provide further documentation concerning the accuracy of the "Pike" dialects, thus suggesting the author's conscious regionalism within his fiction—almost intruding him into the text, since, by this "explanatory," *he* claims the responsibility for styles of speaking in Huck's reports, including the Missouri "Negro" dialect. Before starting to read, the reader is already on notice that he is reading the humorist Twain in his character Huck Finn, altering the reader's sense of the hero accordingly. Twain is reflected in Huck from the beginning. Huck presumably speaks as a child in the young boy's voice, but he introduces us in a sentence using three negatives and connecting the reader to *The Adventures of Tom Sawyer* more than to himself: the book *Tom Sawyer* is his reference, not the person. And Huck is, from the first paragraph, in other ways an adult narrator. He is more consciously self-conscious than a realistic fictional hero would normally be. His second sentence refers to "Mr. Mark Twain," who "told the truth, mainly." And the negatives—which continue—identify Huck as self-effacing in an emotional sense, not merely low-keyed but even self-denying. Yet he also has an adult's experience in lying. Huck refers to several of the characters in both his and Tom Sawyer's books, further-ing our sense of him as an omniscient author rather than a limited character. Couched in a format that suggests some moral pretension—first in the foreword and now in the discussion of lying—the voice of the narrator is closer to Twain the travel writer and Miles Hendon, the hero of *The Prince and the Pauper*, than it is to a barefoot back-woods boy of ten to fourteen.

Huck Finn's dialect is a major contribution to American litera-ture, but the adulthood cloaked in it gives its appeal. Henry Nash Smith has proposed in *Democracy and the Novel* that readers of Henry Ward Beecher's dreadful Civil War novel *Norwood* (1868) were interested less in the book than in becoming fictionally involved with Beecher; Mark Twain's persona in his overall canon—as with most of the literary comedians—produced the same effect for a wide spectrum of American readers. The narrator will be as ironic and self-aware as a character can be who discusses with the reader the previous book in which he appeared. His dialect, with its double and triple negatives, is a mark of vulgarity as well as regionalism. Some colloquial phrases and words appear, but little intrudes. "Stretchers" for "lies" is literary euphemism for comic effect as much as a regional choice; it may be both.

Huck's language establishes his persona and his way of thinking. In the discussion of how much king's "get," the style emphasizes the points: "*They* don't do nothing! Why, how you talk. They just set around." Each dialect word or phrase occurs at a point where it acts both as a language trait and as a social criticism. Other characters—often adults, as in the flatboatmen in chapter 16 or the yokels in chap-ter 41—are more vulgar and ignorant than Huck with more obvious language inflections. But would a fourteen-year-old boy report such variances? The dialect is a Twainian portrayal of his folk region, but is it photographic realism or symbolic realism? Is this its real source of power? Although Huck's simplicity is often praised, his language is a complex creation of Twain's.

Huck's dialect and diction are well represented in the first few paragraphs. Huck's language is colloquial or "vernacular," to use a term familiar to Twain and used by Henry Nash Smith in *Mark Twain: The Development of a Writer* (1962) to interpret Twain's canon. More than that, it is rich in metaphors related not only to the Mississippi River setting of the 1840s but also resonant with the fears of loneliness and death that are particularly haunting to Huck and which give his fear of hell a particular relevance. First, his language sets him off from the conventional educated adult. Huck's "ain't" is the quintessential identifier of vulgar speech; "You don't know about me, without . . . " sounds enough like a double negative to establish the same point. The first six words are also suggestive: the second person "you" is addressed, and "me" is at the object end of the sentence, rather than the subject end, surrounded with negatives about being known. In the second sentence, "mainly" and "stretchers"—carefully used the second time for "lies" after Huck used the verb "stretched"—reinforce the vernacular informality of the language. Huck proceeds cautiously, including in the first paragraph a repetition about lies and the phrase "as I said before." Verbs are miscast in tense to suggest uneducated dialect. Similarly, when Huck says "Tom and me" instead of "Tom and I" our sense of uneducated ignorance is increased. The appearance of naturalness in Huck's story is appealing, but its density of vulgar misusages may have been as galling to critics such as the Concord Library Board as were Huck's ironic attacks on Sunday schools in the following chapters.

Huck is more than uneducated, he is overpoweringly literal, and he is already responding to the paradoxes of freedom and civilization. Partly inverted phrases suggest Huck's literalness: "Tom's Aunt Polly, she is" and "Now the way that the book winds up, is this." He names things first, cautiously, before completing the grammatical sentence: structurally, the formula establishes the trait of mind which will expand into Huck's deadpan humor. With this caution in mind, yet with the dialogue already abstracted to the level of discussing truth and lies, Huck comes immediately to the most abstract level of discussion, his being "sivilized" by the widow Douglas. The misspelling is a device, for which the formal name is cacography. The *s* spelling calls our attention to the term as a generalization and carries an unstated vulgar response to it. Earlier claims about the accuracy of the *spoken* dialect enhance the irony of this gratuitous pretended dialect word; it is literary comedy, not dialect humor. As early as the second paragraph, Huck thus identifies the major issue of the novel. *Adventures of Huckleberry Finn* as a thematic undertaking is well advanced by the end of the first page. "Sivilization"—here connected to widow Douglas—will reappear twice more, connected to Pap Finn, and in the last page of the novel, when Huck restates his intention to escape. Each use reintroduces the theme of escape from civilized control.

Huck's language is important not only as vernacular or colloquial

American English, fresh and in itself a literary event, but rather for the way Twain uses Huck's Pike dialect while developing—very rapidly—issues of social conformity which parallel the grammatical freedom, but at a higher level of personal action. We see Huck "free and satisfied" in his rags and hogshead; we also see Tom's gang of robbers equated with respectability—an allusion to the intrusion of robber barons already apparent in American commercial life. Tom's use of romantic terms is a travesty of the language of adult romances, with the discussion of "ransom" foreshadowing Jim's plight. Praying becomes "grumble a little over the victuals"; eager becomes "in a sweat"; formal restrained drawing-room experience is reinterpreted through the eyes of a character from the village street. To readers who expected a child's book to provide a model of speech and deportment, *Huck Finn* was unpleasantly revolutionary.

However later critics may see the language, it comes to the reader loaded with personalizing humanity. Dialect speech had been prominent in Jack Downing's comic letters by Seba Smith in the 1830s, in James Russell Lowell's *Biglow Papers* in the 1840–1860 period, and in T. C. Haliburton's Yankee clockmaker Sam Slick, as well as in regional sketches found prominently in sporting and literary papers to which Sam Clemens had access. Browne's Artemus Ward letters offered a mixture of dialect and false spellings which involved different levels of irony and character. Since Huck's first-person narrative usually gets credit as the first convincing use of American language in American fiction, a brief comparison may illustrate its actual source of power. George Washington Harris's *Sut Lovingood's Yarns,* written from 1854 on, familiar to Twain, and published in book form in 1867, offers considerable dialect. Sut is young and vulgarly vernacular, like Huck, but a crucial difference lies in Sut's cruelty. Where Huck focuses on escape and his own identity, Sut is antagonistic to others whose values he dislikes. He is not deferential like Huck, but elevates himself above others: "I ain't like ole Glabbergab; when I'se spoke off what I knows, I stops talkin" (New Haven: College & University Press, 1966, 150). The tone is aggressive; the borrowed name is too metaphoric. The language is beyond the delicate comic realism developed by Twain for Huck; it is too realistic. Add to Huck's language the sterner words Twain deleted, and a wider segment of readers might find the supposedly liberating language to diminish their attachment to the vulgar speaker; would Huck be approachable if he talked like Harris's character in "Sut at a Negro Night-Meeting": "A pimpil-face, greasy-collar'd, limber-mouf'd suckit rider drap't ofen a fat hoss, an' sot in tu sorter startin the nigger brethrin in the rite track. He warn't fur frum being a nat'ral born durn'd fool hisself" (130). Huck's dialect is more muted; his irony is lower in key than Sut's open sarcasm, as a reference to the camp meeting described in Huck's voice in chapter 20 will verify.

In longer instances, such as a paragraph in Sut's 1861 journey with "Old Abe," the talk about lynching and beating abolitionists is even stronger:

> Spose the fool killer wer tu kill (as in juty bound he orter) every 'bolitionist now livin; woudent the same sile an climit, an feedin what perjused the d—d ole cusses what burnt ole, palsied wimen as witches; as perjused Jo Smith, an ole Miller, en Miss Fox, and Wendil Phillips, an Missess Bloomer, with her breeches an shut, nex year perjuse just such another crop, say? Ove course hit would, an yet the rich strikes in that ar country ove cod fish an mullen stalks, perjuced a Hancock an the *Day Book*, so emaxulashen wont du; ye must kill em jist as yu ketch em, es yu du your fleas, an rely (es I dus on my laigs) on hard work in follerin arter em frum generashun tu generashun. They onderstand this ere thing in Texas adzactly; give em a black jack and a pece ove bed cord, an that ar all they ax. (246)

Both Artemus Ward and Mark Twain commented (with irony rather than malediction) on the Puritans who hung idiotic old women for witches. Even the flea-metaphor is less prepossessing than Huck's illustrations, as with his reference to hogs in church, for example. Sut is harsh and inhumane; his orientation is toward control through violence. The secret of moral power does not lie in dialect alone. Huck is an observer of right and wrong; when he suffers, he specifically comments that he means no harm to anyone, as when he wishes he was in hell to get relief from Miss Watson's criticisms. As Huck describes events, commonplace activities seemingly without authorial intrusion establish the book's major motifs, as when Huck is taught about Moses and the Bulrushers and finds out that Moses had been dead "a considerable long time; so than I didn't care no more about him; because I don't take no stock in dead people." Huck's matter-of-factness covers a false statement: he is preoccupied with death at the end of that very chapter. In the next paragraph, he describes himself as being seen as having mean and unclean practices, and responds as the deadpan adult which he is, "That is just the way with some people.

They get down on a thing when they don't know nothing about it." Then he weaves back into factuality by describing Miss Watson's use of snuff. Huck on the snakes loosed in Aunt Sally's house is similarly reserved in the face of arrant slap-stick comedy which would have brought out all of Sut's meanness. The result of such speech, which can be traced throughout the novel, is an unusually humane and so-phisticated comic narrator; he pretends to boyishness and innocence, but his naivete is the contrived language of a detached and insightful person. Huck's patience in discomfort adds to the sympathy a reader develops for him.

Chapter 1 of *Adventures of Huckleberry Finn* establishes main themes as well as developing an especially appealing American dialect voice and tone. Civilization, religion, and manners are identified through Huck's life with the widow Douglas and Miss Watson, who immedi-ately become Huck's antagonists. But even in the first chapter Twain's concepts broaden from individual to general and universal. Immedi-ately, Tom Sawyer talks Huck out of his "free and satisfied" state in the woods to be "cramped up" and "worked . . . middling hard" by tight clothes and Miss Watson's unforgiving Christian doctrine. Tom is on the side of the "respectable," for his band of robbers is the lure to get Huck back to the widow; the ironic juxtaposition of robbers and respectability identifies Tom Sawyer's motif for the rest of the novel; in fact, the one sentence aligns Tom with the corrupt Congress of *The Gilded Age* and the nobility in *A Connecticut Yankee*. The last fifth of the book represents the ultimate elaboration of his position, as refined through the next two chapters.

Another central theme is the discussion of the "bad place." After being worked hard by Miss Watson, Huck is lectured about the bad place. With the superficial naïveté of the literary comedian he is, he blurts out that he wishes he were there, not to "mean no harm" but only for a change, "I warn't particular." Huck the pragmatist seeks pleasant experiences. His motif will be ease, where hers is winning success by restricting life. Thus, his response is appropriate to the gog-gle-eyed spinster who lectures him with "don'ts." But even the kindly widow is repressive, as the idea of "free" contrasts with her idea of "respectable." Huck's heart will bring him to the same position when it overpowers his deformed social conscience later. First, "dismal reg-ular" is the opposite of a good stew where "things get all mixed up"; being "cramped up" opposes "free and satisfied" in relaxed clothing and living outdoors; wanting a change to ease from being "worked hard" is "wicked," and the response to verbal abuse on behalf of doctrine is to say nothing "because it would only make trouble and wouldn't do no good,"—showing us Huck the pragmatist in relaxed candor.

The widow Douglas is not untainted, either, in opposition to Huck. Huck's seeming casualness about her taking snuff being "all right, because she done it herself" puts her humorously but firmly in the ranks of the self-centered authoritarian hypocrites who deny him his honesty and liberating flexibility. The rest of the book is devoted to working out these conflicts. Miss Watson, as the slim old maid with goggles on, takes the lead, but the widow also calls Huck a poor lost lamb, and Tom Sawyer is implicated, having contrived Huck's return. Yet Huck himself wants to be with Tom—even if in the bad place; the alternative is a dreadful loneliness, heightened by superstitious fears and thoughts of pain and death. Comic irony is underpinned by this sense of human feeling in Huck; it is the source of his real fear of hell as expressed at the climax of the novel. Since Tom represents community, however falsely constructed, part of Twain's problem in *Huck Finn* will be to distance the reader from Tom while Huck remains devoted to him. The reader must be empowered to reach conclusions about a whole social milieu that remain partly beyond Huck's mental grasp even after the river journey with Jim. In that, Twain will remain a realist.

More is defined than the conflict between the restrictions of manners and the innocent freedom of the boy-hero. The central religious motif of the book is established by bringing in Moses and by elaborating ironically on the themes of heaven, hell, and loneliness. The story of Moses, found in a reed raft on a river, and thereby superficially parallelling Huck's venture, may help establish a theme of orphanage and the development of moral authority, setting a context for Huck, although Huck will never rise to political authority. But Miss Watson's elaboration of the good and bad place lays down the lines for Huck's whole moral adventure—the spiritual conflict and resolution which give his physical adventures their importance. Huck was lured into her control by Tom's offers of adventure and inclusion in the gang, but Miss Watson distorts the action. Her version of heaven is highly restrictive and static, the opposite of anything Mark Twain might subscribe to. Huck's "wicked" preference for the bad place is a preference in favor of freedom from authoritarian control and the manners of the Missouri drawing room. Its opposite is a sense of freedom and friendship—the antidote to the loneliness which Miss Watson forces upon Huck, and its natural outcome: superstitious fear. The last paragraph of chapter 1 achieves this sense when Huck, after killing a spider and fearing the attending bad luck, makes his first melodramatic escape. He scrambles out his darkened window and joins Tom Sawyer in the woods outside the widow's darkened house. All readers share the brief exaltation and release of the moment, and it needs no didactic elaboration by Twain; Jim and Huck will replay the act of rejoining several times before Tom Sawyer reenters and we achieve the last reprise in the final chapter of the novel.

The first use of the racial epithet "nigger" appears in chapter 1 when Huck says, "By and by they fetched in the niggers and had prayers." The actual word appears roughly 200 times in the course of the novel. Although "nigger" was more casually used in Twain's day, even in the nineteenth century sensitive whites found it offensive and degrading. In J. T. Trowbridge's *A Picture of the Desolated States; and the Work of Restoration, 1865–1868* (Hartford, Conn.: L. Stebbens, 1868), "nigger" is used throughout the record of the journalist's travels through the South, but only in reported speech and anecdotes characterizing southerners interviewed by Trowbridge. The word is an indicator of racial antagonism. Trowbridge in his own vocabulary uses "black," "freedman," or "slave"; as the text winds on, the interplay of Trowbridge's sensitivity with regional attitudes is heightened. *Cudjo's Cave* (1864) shows an application corresponding to *Huck Finn*. Twain, a decade later, understood the potential in the word, and he used it to heighten the same contrast, although he would not, in a first-person realist novel, discuss the point and transform it into didacticism.

Appropriate to Twain's intention, the word "nigger" shows up very densely in a few locations. Take the whole sentence or segment of the novel surrounding its use and its irony appears. The juxtaposition of the epithet with the idea of prayers is an obvious case of irony, although seldom discussed. Pap Finn's chapter uses the word particularly often, as do the minstrel-style arguments between Huck and Jim where the degraded attitude of the regional mind (for which we might say "limited" rather than "southern") uses "nigger" as the *ad hominem* shift in logical reasoning; Huck laments that he can't teach a "nigger" to argue when beaten by logical illogic. Some phrases, like

"Give a nigger an inch and he'll take an ell," are intended to suggest the bad effects of local thought on a good mind like Huck's. They are introduced to make the reader uncomfortable. The ultimate device is the gratuitous response to Aunt Sally when she asks if anyone was hurt in the steamboat explosion: "No'm, killed a nigger."

Many black readers find the use of the word "nigger" as oppressive as they find the portraiture of Jim. Jim adheres to many of the values of his society. After all, Twain could have muted his portrait. That he did not is evidence of his sense of its centrality to his message. He might change, and did change, "drunk" to "mellow" on occasion because the problem of temperance was not his foremost issue, and a comic softening was therefore appropriate. Even Clara Clemens introduced a joint edition of *Huck Finn* and *Tom Sawyer* (New York: Platt & Munk, 1960) with a Twain comment speaking to the issue: "I am quite sure that (bar one) I have no race prejudices, and I think I have no color prejudices nor caste prejudices. Indeed I know it. I can stand any society. All I care about is that a man is a human being." In discussing dialects in the book, he uses the word "Negro" in the preface. Realism dictated that he create a real-seeming language that carried its own condemnation of bigotry. He intended to be aggressive in putting forth the most blatant symbol of that American and universal shortcoming; here, it is "nigger." It is a sorry fact that the word and the portrait is a troubling one to young black readers, as it must be. It is an even sorrier fact that condemning the book for its portrait is merely killing the messenger who brings the bad news. Purging the portrait will not change human nature, nor would Twain have tolerated such an argument for shirking the test of virtue which the word represents. As a literary artist, he uses it to increase our frustration with what it represents until the "No'm, killed a nigger" speech, Tom's coat of arms, and the Doctor's supposedly kind speech toward Jim at the end of the evasion. Black readers will feel a personalized sense of disgust, but sensitive white readers share at least the literary, if not the fully internalized personal, ramifications.

When Huck is reunited with Tom Sawyer in chapter 2 and they undertake pranks on Jim and the establishment of a robber gang, the novel ostensibly returns to the popular format of the nostalgic boy's book. Twain used this format in *The Adventures of Tom Sawyer,* and a number of authors had also successfully practiced it, including T. A. Henty, J. T. Trowbridge, and Horatio Alger. The model was that plaguey boy Ike, Mrs. Partington's mischievous child in B. P. Shillaber's tales in the Boston *Carpet-Bag* in the 1840s and later. Thomas Bailey Aldrich's *The Story of a Bad Boy,* which attained great popularity in 1869, stimulated Twain as well. According to Alan Gribben, Twain's motivation was partly resentment because he felt intruded on by Aldrich's efforts in the local color of "Rivermouth," the New England small town presented as the setting for his youthful "bad boy" escapades and pranks.[9] Twain, Professor Gribben notes, started to mark Aldrich's book for Livy in 1869 during their courting, but complained that he finally could not admire it much. Twain's Hannibal, Missouri, must have seemed a richer source of local color to him. Aldrich's bad boy and Twain's Tom Sawyer were both presented as "real" boys, at least, in distinction to the didactic fiction which sought to "exhibit the beauty of goodness and virtue so entwined in the thread of every story, as to render unnecessary a dry moral at the end for the children to skip, as they invariably do," to cite the words of one "Aunt Fanny" (Mrs. F. E. M. Barrow) in her *Nightcaps,* a children's book from earlier in the nineteenth century (circa 1855).

Another energizing influence on Twain's emotional investment in *Huck Finn* as a boy's book was undoubtedly the spirit of the times. Henry Ward Beecher, the most influential liberal theologian in America during the 1850–1870 period, had taken strong positions advocating the development of real boy literature. Beecher's church had sponsored the Quaker City voyage that resulted in Twain's *Innocents Abroad,* and Twain was interested in Beecher's sermons. As early as 1857, Beecher, already prominent as a Protestant Romantic espousing naturalness in religion, called for dramatic truth in childhood literature. "City Boys in the Country," a column in the New York *Ledger* in 1857, was important enough to him to be reprinted in a book of essays titled *Eyes and Ears* (Boston: Ticknor & Fields, 1862). Beecher announced his hope for the book "to inspire a love of Nature, or an enjoyment of rural occupations, or to form a kindly habit of judging men and events." In the essay he contended that a boy was a piece of existence quite separate from the man: "The real lives of boys are yet to be written, . . . the lives of pious and good boys . . . resemble a real boy's life about as much as a chicken picked and larded, upon a spit, and ready for delicious eating, resembles a free fowl in the fields." He expanded on this idea by calling good-boy piety "monstrous" and a pâté de foie gras piety. Such sentiments speak strongly to the kind of motivation Twain must have felt to retrieve a real backwoods persona from his Missouri childhood. It is noteworthy to find a leading American theologian advocating the course Twain later followed; as unconventional as Huck seems, he is a more natural product of Twain's America than at first meets the eye.

Nor did Beecher stop with the condemnation in general of the unnaturalness of the children of the religious society tracts. He described real boys as meddlesome, inquisitive, and disruptive of order, battling both baths and good manners, a further precedent for the conflict between Huck and the widow and Miss Watson. Beecher notes not only that boys speak out of order but continues that "they will tell lies," thus endorsing another motif in the opening of the novel. As a liberal, Beecher suggests string, a knife, and pencil and paper—since boys aspire to do what men do indoors—and a safe stream of water outdoors; repression is not suggested. So Beecher even provides the river motif, a happy coincidence of relationships which figure equally importantly in Twain's personal experience of the Mississippi. Most important of all, Beecher declares that time spent in the country will ensure moral growth to adulthood, for "The country is appointed of God to be the children's nursery; the city seems to have been made by malign spirits to destroy children in." Twain's vision of Huck and the river was responsive to this doctrine. Later books promulgated by the philanthropic children's aid societies, such as George C. Needham's *Street Arabs and Gutter Snipes* (Philadelphia: Hubbard Bros., 1888) show this philosophy to have become a major social program; reformist books featuring the lights and shadows of city-child life show that Twain's portrait of Huck has far more precedent in American social thought than a naive reader might assume, or than the Concord Library Board took into account in responding to the surface melodrama of its plot and the veneer of Huck's behavior.

Beecher's analysis is important because he looks to the ethical and moral growth of the child. As Twain was to demonstrate in *Adventures of Huckleberry Finn,* Beecher contends that he has not heard "one moral problem discussed in later life that is not questioned by children. . . . Indeed, all truths whose root and life are in the Infinite are like the fixed stars, which become no larger under the most powerful telescope than to the natural eye." Moreover, as shown in Huck and reiterated in Huck's sense of Jim, boys are identified in Beecher's analysis as having hours of "great sinking and sadness"—the first of which has already come to Huck at the end of chapter 1—when "kindness and fondness are peculiarly needful to them," of the sort Jim and Mary Jane Wilks will offer Huck. At the climax of the novel, Huck will be particularly responsive to this truth as he reviews all the past kindnesses of the adult Jim to him on the raft. Although some critics complain that Jim acts like an old plantation darkie, Jim seems to fulfill Beecher's calls for sympathetic parental nurturing.

In opposition to the positive suggestions given above, Beecher also comments on the style of a Miss Watson, in effect. He complains that it is remarkable that boys overcome the badgering and scolding, as well as the flattering and indulgence, to which children are subjected: "Human nature has an element of great toughness in it. When we see what men are made of, our wonder is, not that so many children are spoiled, but that so many are saved." Huck's rejection of the heaven and hell of a nagging Miss Watson, at the same time that he maintains a fear of it, seems reasonable in light of Beecher's analysis.

A blueprint for the character of Huckleberry Finn is laid out in Beecher's "City Boys in the Country." Huck's sadness, his need for kindness and acceptance, his ability to allow natural morality to overcome corrupting false doctrines nagged into him by a selfish society, all are characteristics that have remained most attractive to readers of the book. Civil War and post–Civil War America was strongly predisposed to follow Beecher's viewpoint and respect the natural dignity and potential moral development of its children. Huck himself may have come as a revelation to readers in 1885, but the undergirding philosophy was already in place.

The boy's book format only works for two or three chapters, although its reenactment in the book's final eleven chapters, from 32 through Chapter the Last, is based on the conflict between the naive and the sophisticated views of boy life as represented by Tom and Huck. The melodramatic return of Pap Finn ends any pretense to a light view of childhood. Even so, it might be argued that Twain burlesques not only the didactic good boy's book but goes one step further, a very important step in elevating *Huck Finn* to the level of visionary literature, by debunking the pretentious bad boy's book as well. Even in chapter 1, Tom Sawyer is condemned by Miss Watson to go to the other place than heaven, but Miss Watson, from the first, is a tainted witness. Tom's seduction of Huck back into the nagging captivity and restrictive clothing of the village (city) life of widow Douglas and Miss Watson makes a central distinction between them. Tom's allegiance as of chapter 1 is not with Huck but with the village world against Huck's natural world. Chapters 2 and 3 expand their differences, showing Tom to be an authoritarian at war with naturalness.

Undermining Authority

A final point is worth making about Mark Twain and Huck Finn as personae. At least one fugitive paragraph in 1885 linked the two directly, and since the source is Sam Clemens's mother, the remark might be helpful in proposing a direct link between author and character. Mrs. Clemens was interviewed in Keokuk, Iowa, as reported in *The Critic* of 12 December 1885:

> "Sam was always a good-hearted boy," said Mrs. Clemens; "but he was a very wild and mischievous one, and, do what we would, we could never make him go to school. This used to trouble his father and me dreadfully, and we were convinced that he would never amount to as much in the world as his brothers, because he was not near so steady and sober-minded as they were." "I suppose, Mrs. Clemens, that your son in his boyhood days somewhat resembled his own Tom Sawyer, and that a fellow-feeling is what made him so kind to the many hair-breadth escapades of that celebrated youth?" "Ah, no!" replied the old lady, with a merry twinkle in her eye; "he was more like Huckleberry Finn than Tom Sawyer. Often his father would start him off to school, and in a little while would follow him to ascertain his whereabouts. There was a large stump on the way to the school-house, and Sam would take his position behind that, and as his father went past would gradually circle around it in such a way as to keep out of sight. Finally his father and teacher both said it was no use to try to teach Sam anything, because he was determined not to learn. But I never gave up. He was always a great boy for history, and would never get tired of that kind of reading; but he hadn't any use for school-houses and textbooks."

Connecting a threatening father with trips to school is a helpful linking of personality traits in the real and the fictional character. The bare statement that Sam was a Huck rather than a Tom, whether strictly true or not, substantiates the divergences in motive which Twain paints into the first three chapters of the later novel. Combine this personality with the real boy from Hannibal named Tom Blankenship, as identified in *Mark Twain's Autobiography* (1961) and elsewhere, who once befriended a runaway Negro slave, and the elements of the story are almost complete. Tom is closer to the fictional bad boy comic figure; Huck is closer to real motivations admired by young Sam. Add the visionary conception of heart overcoming conscience, as Twain himself summarized his motive in his 1895 notebooks and also add the real boy-runaway slave episode of Tom Blankenship in Hannibal as identified by Dixon Wecter, and the skeleton of the novel is complete.

Chapters 2 and 3, although written in the boy's book manner, break into the higher level of vision that Twain developed in seeing in boy life, as did Beecher, a means to higher and more natural truth, realistically experienced. As Tom plays a trick on Miss Watson's Jim, develops a robber gang, discusses ransoms, and manipulates his friends by hoked up distortions of romance, he encounters opposition from Huck and the other boys. Likewise, as Miss Watson attempts to dictate Huck's religious faith, his natural curiosity brings him to connect her doctrines with Tom Sawyer's lies—profound developments this early in the novel.

At the opening of chapter 2, Tom contrives a situation which reasserts Huck's loneliness and isolation, while introducing us to "Miss Watson's big nigger, named Jim." Tom determines, over Huck's protests, to steal candles, for which Tom then pays. This act establishes that Huck fears punishment while Tom ignores his reasonable caution, and that Tom honors established rules of ownership by paying for what he takes; Tom is indeed the good bad boy acceptable to his society. Furthermore, Tom must also play "something" on Jim. The result, narrated in Huck's deadpan voice, is that Jim is "looked up to" by other "niggers," based on his comically exaggerated story of a witch's ride, but is "stuck up" and "most ruined" as a servant. Jim is set in his milieu; the motif will be tremendously expanded in the ending of the novel. The most important consequences of Tom's little escapade, even before we see Huck and Tom together with Tom's gang, are in further isolating Huck, and the metaphors used are social ones. Lying in the dark at Jim's feet, the unwilling Huck provides us with a slapstick narration of itching while not being able to scratch—a favorite Twain theme that would be a springboard for imagining a Connecticut Yankee stuck in Arthurian armor, later elaborated into another novel. For Huck, the observance is that this occurs "with the quality, or at a funeral"; Tom has brought Huck right back into the repressions of the village. At the end of the little sequence, Huck waits for Tom to complete his joke and notices that everything seemed "so still and lonesome." Rejoined with his friend, Huck still experiences isolation rather than sympathetic unity: his relationship to come with Jim will reverse this action in the real separation and real uniting of sympathy after Huck's playing his joke on Jim during the fog.

Undermining Authority

After a lengthy paragraph of purposely "low" humor, the great theme of the river is offered to us for the first time—an offering easy to read over without consciously noticing, but nonetheless important. In one paragraph the word "nigger" appears seven times, identifying that paragraph as one which stamps a lowered image of either the Negro or the speaker. The action of the paragraph is consistent with Tom's calculated degradation of Jim by his joke. Jim is reduced to the role of comic darkie. As an alternative, even as Huck and Tom link up with Jo Harper and Ben Rogers to form the gang, Huck, connecting sickness and sadness with the towns, looks out at the grandeur of the river—an alternative which he will pursue, and which will be dignified at its highest moment by a long elaboration of this brief night scene in chapter 19. Here, on the hill-top, Huck "could see three or four lights twinkling, where there was sick folks, may be; and the stars over us was sparkling ever so fine; and down by the village was the river, a whole mile broad, and awful still and grand." Dialectal markers like "awful" and the misused "was" barely disguise the very unvernacular sublimity of this first great view of the river.

Tom's creation of a band of robbers in chapter 2 provides us with a travesty of the sources he relies on. Heavily developed throughout even this innocent-seeming activity is the theme of Tom's half-baked, rigid, and self-serving distortion of authorities to maintain his control over others. Sunday maintains its importance as well; the boys conclude by agreeing that it would be wicked to meet on Sunday, thus acknowledging their subservience to the world of Miss Watson. The chapter thus implicates romantic novels, Tom, and village religion as repressive intrusions on real boy life. All the elaborations of Huck's admiration for Tom later in the book are shaded by the depiction of Tom in chapter 2.

Tom Sawyer's formation of the gang completes the undermining of his character for us as readers. Tom's special knowledge of a hidden cave entrance partially validates his egocentric naming of the gang after himself, but only partly. The first indication of travesty is in the pledge that members breaching the oath will first be "sued," dragging in village law, and then be killed in retaliation; the idea that every "high toned" gang had a bloody oath also vaguely suggests a comic reference to adult corporate life. Further travesty occurs in the attempt to be stylish, always Tom Sawyer's theme relating him to social admiration, by becoming highwaymen rather than common burglars who only steal cattle. Even worse, at the end of the robber-gang sequence, Tom will bribe little Tommy Barnes with five cents not to tell of the gang, thus showing himself even less prepossessing than before. Tom reflects the Gilded Age; he is no moral model for us, but for different reasons than Miss Watson would reject. Since the portraiture is humorous, the differentiation between what the characters concluded about each other and what we conclude must lead us to see how ardently Twain champions Huck's will to spiritual freedom against Tom's spiritual corruption.

Undermining Tom is his willful perversion of even the rigid authorities, shown here in relation to the idea of "ransom." He emphasizes that the gang has "*got*" to do what's "in the books." But he guesses that keeping people till they are ransomed means keeping them until they are dead. One of the boys wonders why captives can't be ransomed with a club as soon as they are captured. A casual reader will see this interchange as mere boy fun, but the travesty is given more weight when compared to chapter 19 of *A Connecticut Yankee,* where the Yankee describes the wicked Morgan le Fay as rushing to "photograph" prisoners with an ax. For the Yankee, the interpretation of an unknown word as a murderous one shows an underlying violence that was "sharply characteristic." The boys complain that Tom's goody-goody treatment of female prisoners is a "fool way, anyhow," but he sticks to it, contending that more practical ways "ain't in the books so." Tom has even debated the opinions of the "authorities" with himself; explicit use of that word suggests how he takes the authoritarian position, the "correct"view, even when distorting the rules. His romance seems as perverse as Miss Watson's religion to us and to Huck. These motifs will expand in the last chapters; but Twain has created enough negative implications even here in chapter 2 to prejudice a reader against the later plans Tom will bring forth.

Chapter 2 distances Huck from the rest of the gang by distinguishing him as the only boy who has no proper "family." Exaggerated importance is given to this element through the burlesque threats of burning ashes, death, kidnapping, and blood. "Everybody" must have kin to punish for disloyalty; every boy except Huck is thus closely linked to the town. Huck's Pap "used to lay drunk with the hogs in the tanyard, but he ain't been seen" for a year. The tanyard reference is the sort of reference that critics picked out to show the degraded character of the novel; its implication is realistic, suggesting a social lowering of Huck's place. Huck will ultimately share even more of Pap's alienated character, but now he is only spared tears by offering the gang Miss Watson to kill. Such irony in Artemus Ward the old showman was the hypocrisy of the coward; in Huck it is the irony of a detached outcast.

By the end of chapter 2, Huck Finn's motifs have been established, particularly the conflict between authority and freedom. Tom has already been separated from Huck in being closer to family and town, whereas Huck must be lured back to town from his rags, must be compelled to play pranks which exploit Jim, and is set off and isolated with his own feelings of loneliness and fear of death by Miss Watson's nagging, the widow Douglas's confining bedroom, and Tom's authorities. When Ben Rogers says "I don't take no stock in it" regarding Tom's plans, he reechoes Huck's not taking stock in dead people, reemphasizing the failure of Miss Watson's religion and Tom's romantic fantasy alike to supply significant matter to a real boy. Miss Watson informed us that Tom Sawyer would go to hell, but we know this is false; it is misleading information which Huck will truly supplant.

With the two providences speech in chapter 3, religious authority is given a formal identification in relation to Huck Finn's own status as a person. Twain's visionary level of discourse is thus put in place within the localized development of the plot concerning Huck, Tom, the townspeople, and Pap. Jim does not yet enter into the creation of the higher levels of the plot; he is still a localized character, although Huck's description of his behavior "afterwards" has already implied that he has broader standing in the novel than other characters. In addition to the two providences speech Huck explicitly identifies Tom's play authorities with lying and Sunday schools. Most important, even as early as chapter 3, the reader is exposed to the dynamism that binds Miss Watson, Tom, and Pap together in opposition to Huck the easy pragmatist.

Huck's two providences speech occurs in an extended review of the doctrine of gifts, loosely defined. The argument is as sophisticated as his speech, although both are presented in vernacular dialect. Light touches of religion infuse the moment. He apologizes for the widow's calling him a "lost lamb" with the mild Twainian irony that she "didn't mean no harm by it." When he comments on the uselessness of Tom Sawyer's games, he says you could polish fake swords until you rotted and they "wouldn't amount to a mouthful of ashes," a biblical-sounding phrase. In fact, Twain makes the last two words of the chapter "Sunday school," in this case a negative reference, like much of

Beecher's commentary on orthodox religion. The context for Huck as backwoods theologian is intensely religious—perhaps a reflection of milieu, but more likely a reflection of Twain's moral mind in action. In fact, Twain's own sense of the adulthood of Huck's musings may have caused him to have Huck specify that it was good enough to "make a *boy's* mouth water" (my italics) when describing his response to the widow's depiction of heaven.

Chapter 3 opens with the widow sorrowing over Huck passively and Miss Watson taking him into a closet—another image of repression, certainly—to pray. Her doctrine of gifts seems to identify "spiritual gifts" with getting advantages "for the other people." Huck the pragmatist prays and gets a fishline but no hooks. His self-oriented and immediate test is denounced as "foolish" by her. Significantly, when Tom's gang busts up the Sunday school picnic, they "never got anything but some doughnuts and jam. . . . I didn't see no di'monds." Tom's fancies are similarly unproductive. Huck's arguments cause Tom to call him "ignorant"; earlier Miss Watson had called him "a fool." Authorities all relate to Huck in the same manner. Widow Douglas, however, represents a positive component of Huck's religiousness; she does not mean any harm—she thus foreshadows Huck and Jim's ethic. In chapter 4, the widow will give Huck his first important endorsement, acknowledging that he was "coming along slow but sure . . . doing very satisfactory. She said she warn't ashamed of me." A motif is established concerning women's ability to recognize Huck's humanity; Mrs. Loftus will later respond to him, and Mary Jane Wilks's respect for Huck and responsiveness to him will fulfill this aspect of the book. Huck's own sense of "shame" is identified, in reflex, for the first time.

A study of the language of chapter 3 shows a second strong element in Huck's response to the authorities. The widow Douglas explains the doctrine of "spiritual gifts" to Huck. It won't retrieve money lost on pork, or silver snuff boxes; therefore, it will not undo literal losses. Her teaching will cause Huck to think about other people all the time and to help them rather than himself—a character trait that is remarkably close to Huck's style later. In response, he retreats "to the woods" and examines the good of this—prayer literally not helping Miss Watson "fat up" but "including Miss Watson, as I took it," his primary antagonist, in the general goodness. Huck announces to the reader, with his usual half-musing, half-explanatory pose, that he "reckoned" he would not worry about it, but "just let it go." Like

Twain's mock Notice and Huck's statement that he don't take no stock in dead people, this is another misdirection. As a technique, misdirection by now has become so common that it must be seen as a major part of Twain's comic method—his device for distancing his spokesman from society ironically. Huck sets up comic oppositions; later, he will crash through them in action.

Huck's major ethical decisions are foreshadowed in the center of chapter 3, establishing a motif of choices that will be reechoed in chapter 31 in Huck's greatest speech when he chooses between heaven and hell for Jim. Huck sees that there are two providences: the widow's is kindly and might take him, but if Miss Watson's "got him," a phrase suggesting vicious animal capture, "there warn't no help for him any more," in its proposed suffering. The conflict between authorities will be elaborated later, leading to Huck's own decision between "two" choices. Early, it is part of the moral structure to be completed with Pap Finn's "Call this a govment" speech in chapter 6. Chapter 3 establishes interconnections and foreshadows moral action with these other crucial speeches in several different ways, both explicitly and by implication. Explicitly, the relation of Huck to salvation in heaven, including his lowdown and ornery nature, becomes a central part of his decision to free Jim, all considered in terms of a harsh Providence—and Jim is, indeed, Miss Watson's, not the widow Douglas's. Implicitly, the speech is linked by various words to Huck's life. The widow Douglas's Providence would "make a boy's mouth water"—the next such sensuous moment will be on Jackson's Island when Huck and Jim prepare a rich dinner together. The concept of "two" providences will be echoed and expanded, both by plot and action, when Huck has to decide forever "betwixt two things" in opting to save Jim and go to hell. Finally, the next person named after this discussion—seemingly out of thin air—is Pap. In fact, "Pap" is the opening word of the following paragraph, allied to the restriction of religion not by belief but by juxtaposition in the stream of the narrative. Such a subtlety is crucial in defining fully what Huck's readers will finally sense as "sivilization" and helps us define his victory at the end of the book.

Huck's rejection of Tom's robber gang, along with the other boys, in chapter 3, also identifies his spirit as especially consistent with American enterprise in the later nineteenth century. When Miss Watson is to be advantaged by "spiritual gifts," Huck—out in the woods turning it over in his own mind—"couldn't see no advantage about it—except for the other people." Couched again in the bad grammar of the illiterate, the sentiment is presumably not for the instruction of the young; it is the reflection of a real boy's mind—a higher form of reality consistent with Beecher's pronouncements and antagonistic to the Concord Library Board. To the religiously conservative, it must have appeared as an attack on orthodoxy—the same attack Twain would mount in "Was it Heaven? or Hell?" and a number of other stories. As pragmatism, however, the sentiment is businesslike and much within the spirit of entrepreneurship as advanced in Howells's *The Rise of Silas Lapham* or John Hay's *The Bread-Winners*, both of which prefer the hands-on activist to either aesthetes or criminals. Huck backs away from hogs as "ingots" and turnips as "julery," to the reader an obvious travesty of romantic sources. He responds to the romance of blazing stick "slogans" with a characteristic comment: "I couldn't see no profit in it."

In case the businessman in Huck were not clear enough, Huck applies the test of labor for profit to Tom's appeal to *Don Quixote*. Huck will get genies to fight other genies by hiring them, just as Silas Lapham would fight a rival paint concern. Further, he understands power, just as Hay broods that his uppercrust Clevelanders do not. Huck says that he, as a forty-foot-tall genie, would see a man in Jericho before he would dump his business for a rubbed tin lamp, and if he did come, he would make the man climb a tree. Huck again retreats to the woods—this time to rub a lamp—testing Tom just as he had earlier tested Miss Watson—again in business terms, "calculating to build a palace and sell it," like any good real estate promoter. When Huck fails, "I judged that all that stuff was only just one of Tom Sawyer's lies. . . . It had all the marks of a Sunday school." Here Huck clearly allies Tom's romance with the town's religion. The novel is already moving in a subversive direction, but advocating a businesslike approach to life, action, and morality, and using that approach to distance Huck from those around him. With the exception of Pap, all of Huck's antagonists are connected by chapter 3 of the novel—and Pap dominates chapters 4 through 7. Tom has been placed above Huck in chapter 1 but his standing is undermined in chapter 3; the flow of the plot has allowed Twain to establish a paradoxical acceptance and rejection of Tom, which the reader must resolve for himself at the end of the book. The mind of Twain the author is embodied fully in these opening chapters. The book functions as an intellectual progression more than as a developing adventure. The real adventure part of the plot will be started later.

When Pap melodramatically enters the novel in chapter 4, he provides Huck with a terrifying personal antagonist. He adds a broadly political-social dimension to Miss Watson's behavioral and religious oppression and to Tom's attempt to control him through the travesty of romantic authorities. Pap's entry is a reentry in many ways, for his appearance has been heavily foreshadowed. His absence almost prevented Huck from being included in Tom Sawyer's gang—an unhappy separation akin to the loneliness of mannerly life. Pap is mentioned again after the two providences speech. Huck describes himself as "comfortable" when Pap is gone and also notes that he would "take to the woods" if Pap returned—his regular pattern of retreat from civilization as announced at the end of *Tom Sawyer* and reiterated in puzzling over "sivilization" in *Huck Finn*. Huck, however, is again "uncomfortable," this time because his folk wisdom, here in burlesque, tells him that the faceless dead body found in the river and thought to be Pap is really a woman in man's clothing. The mood surrounding Pap is already grim, and his reappearance predicted. Pap's reappearance is further denoted as bad luck when Huck spills salt, and Miss Watson—notice again the conjunction between Miss Watson and Pap—prevents Huck from throwing it over his shoulder. His next experience is to discover Pap's bootprint in the snow outside the cottage, marked with a cross to keep off the devil. The references to Pap are couched in a setting of religion and superstition. Pap's malevolence will color our feelings for such superrational beliefs.

Chapter 4 gives a well-focused portrait of Huck. As with dead people, Huck, mismultiplying six times seven, "don't take no stock in mathematics." Ironically, he demonstrates the opposite of what he claims. He immediately rushes to Judge Thatcher, refusing to explain his problem, as is his special heroic characteristic, and contrives for the Judge to set up an artificial sale of Huck's $6,000 property to the judge. Huck is thus effective in shedding the money problem, despite his disclaimer about mathematics. The judge, notably, manipulates legal terms on Huck's behalf, the first of a number of professional types who will act sympathetically toward him. Huck, having so easily disposed of his property to the Judge, seeks counsel with Jim and the hair ball—using a counterfeit quarter—about his future. Huck does not tell Jim that he has Thatcher's dollar; Jim and Huck conspire to cheat the hair ball in the burlesque fortune-telling episode, and Jim offers a travesty of the duplicitous speeches of fortune-telling oracles. With talk of "two" angels, like two providences, hovering around Huck, Jim ends on a non sequitur, keep away from water because you will get hung, which has its own kind of odd implication that Huck should save himself for his own fate. The further irony is that Huck and Jim will soon engage in an extended and danger-fraught raft journey in which their drowning is possible at least twice. Pap will shortly bring Huck the dark angel, the "Angel of Death," in his delirium tremens in chapter 6. Twain the melodramatist foreshadows coming violent action; superstition is used to suggest without exactly predicting future dark events.

Chapters 5 and 6 develop Pap as an antagonist to Huck. Pap is a degraded character, and his appearance and demeanor figured heavily in the contemporary assessments of *Huck Finn* as a bad book showing bad examples of humanity. His drunkenness and violence melodramatically threaten Huck's education and finally disrupt it, and they later threaten his life. His attack on Negroes and the government expands his degradation into a broader context. His ferocity outweighs Miss Watson's, even though his scope in the book is circumscribed by his own opposition to the manners that restrict Huck. He adds ignorance and political hypocrisy to the social dimensions already established. Ultimately, however, Pap is capable of joining with the town for his own advantage; he manipulates the justice system, and he finally joins the townspeople on the steamboat searching for Huck's body. Huck, now further alienated, must flee for his life.

Huck's description of Pap heightens the horror of his entrance even as Twain uses Huck's voice to downplay Huck's supposed fear "after the first jolt." Again, a major pattern is established. Huck tells us that he has developed beyond his earlier fear and now "warn't scared of him worth bothering about." Twain is thus free to develop a whole new level of compelling fear from a more mature standard of life and death.

The action in which Huck abandons his $6,000 does not correspond to the later statement. It was a demonstration of the "earlier" Huck—this is the "later," a character who is capable of maturing in his emotional understanding in regards to others, particularly in the book's central action with Jim. Thus, even Huck and Pap's meeting foreshadows the book's main action of moral growth, which will be expanded on the river.

Pap's degradation establishes an antihumane position that represents the opposite position from the children's aid societies reforming post–Civil War America. First, of course, he is physically repulsive. Pap's white skin is not like another man's, but is a flesh-crawling "tree-toad white, a fish-belly white": images normal for Huck as a resorter to nature for imagery and thought and to the river for escape, but gruesome, and made more so when Pap's hair is described as prison-like vines. The further description of Pap's clothes establishes the damaged shoes and hat that Twain will develop into a retribution for Pap's malevolence in the "call this a govment" speech. Pap "goes for" Huck, as a direct antagonist. He tries to stop his school-going and Huck continues to spite him—further evidence of Huck's opposition to authority corresponding to his response to Miss Watson. Pap angrily accuses Huck of putting on airs, attacks his learning, "whacking" out of his hand a reading on Washington, and then identifies Huck's family in negatives—a mother who never learned to read nor write and then died, and further family who died. He tears up Huck's award and threatens to beat him; next, he demands the money which Huck has just transferred to Judge Thatcher, clarifying for us Huck's device and Pap's own selfish interest in Huck. Last, he takes Huck's dollar and gets drunk. Altogether, Pap is everything loathsome in the calculated abuse of youth, a damning element to genteel censors. The remainder of the chapter is given over to showing an ineffectual "new" judge rendering the law helpless. Pap's level of violence is frightening; his ability to deceive the judge is a criticism of courts that are too passive to intervene for the obvious welfare of the child. Sympathetic middle-class Americans encountered equally awful situations in such books as *Street Arabs,* already mentioned, to spur through literal reportage their demand for social reform.[10] Here the medium is fiction, but the emotion harnessed is the same.

Pap's manipulation of the law offers a distressing example of justice, which Twain purposefully mutes in a comic drunk scene, "reforming the drunkard." The brief episode distances governmental power from Huck's case when the "new" judge refuses to take a child away from its father. Pap is a weakly venal creature who cannot stop his hand from being "the hand of a hog" even when he is given clean clothes, a beautiful room, and womanly kisses. The camp-meeting episode will repeat this moment more broadly, carrying its echoes to a larger area of the plot. At this point, Pap continues to get drunk and, destroying the room in which he has been left, falls down and breaks his arm. Huck's dryness, "He was just suited—this kind of thing was right in his line," is the irony of the mature reporter turned fiction writer. Poetic justice allows immediate retribution in Pap's fall.

The new judge episode introduces us to the governmental action that triggers Pap's attack on the "govment." First the widow and the judge respond to Pap's bullyragging Thatcher—another foreshadowing moment expanded in the Boggs-Sherburn episode—by attempting to become Huck's guardians. Seeking to aid Huck, they are rejected by the legal agency that should help them: government is as incapacitated to rescue a child as religion is to secure immediate physical benefit. Pap in turn sues Judge Thatcher for Huck's $6,000, and simultaneously takes direct action by getting drunk on the money that Thatcher is still passing on to Huck. Finally, Pap kidnaps Huck, thus showing him who is "Huck Finn's boss." Pap's casual violence is suggested in comic detachment by Huck: Pap "got drunk and had a good time, and licked me," again using the subdued ironic voice of a literary comedian.

Huck's kidnapping by Pap establishes an alternative to the smothery loneliness of the town. Times across the river are "lazy and jolly." Rules are not maintained; clothes become rags; swearing is not repressed. "Smoking and fishing, and no books nor study" define the summertime ideal of this new breed of boy's books which, written by middle-class professionals for other middle-class readers, elevated the concept of pure leisure. Of course, Miss Watson "pecking at you" provides an alternative reference. Within a paragraph, however, Huck describes Pap as "too handy with his hick'ry"—physical punishment has now replaced mental cruelty. Locking Huck in for three days at a time, Pap leaves Huck again "dredful lonesome"—with the net effect of Miss Watson's pecking, although much more physically threatening. Huck conducts a detailed search and makes plans for escape; the cabin, it seems, is connected to the village, but is even worse. Pap returns to Huck in a bad humor—"so he was his natural self," the laconic reporter's voice tells us—with further tales of his struggles with the law. Two paragraphs of discussion again connect Pap and the town as antagonists to Huck. The widow is suing for guardianship, shaking Huck because he doesn't want to "be so cramped up and sivilized." Pap threatens to stow Huck six or seven miles away, and Huck says, "That made me pretty uneasy again." So both parties make Huck uneasy, justifying his plans to escape from both before he is subjected to more talk of damnation or more welts. Immediately following is Pap's "call this a govment" speech, one of the most important speeches in the book.

Pap is shown drinking, swearing, and covered with mud—"a body would a thought he was Adam," says Huck, as Twain packs yet another biblical allusion into the texture of the prose, connecting Pap with religion almost as much as Miss Watson is connected by her overt moralizing. Then comes one of the book's early highpoints, Pap's attack on the "govment" and near murder of Huck in delirium tremens. The first paragraph of Pap's "call this a govment" speech demands his "rights." To Pap, Huck's $6,000 becomes his rightful property, and Judge Thatcher's manipulations are a violation of his rights—as he claims to have told the judge "right to his face" in action that is later duplicated by Boggs and Sherburn. He talks in the manner of a good but distressed 1880s parent, however ironically, describing himself as having had the "anxiety and all the expense" of raising Huck to a point where Huck could now do something for him. He decries his flap-lidded beat-up stovepipe hat—worn by "one of the wealthiest men in this town, if I could get my rights." The next point in the novel where the reader will encounter such demands for "rights" will be aboard the *Walter Scott,* again with thieves and rapscallions making the demands.

Having labeled this sequence himself, Pap starts a second paragraph of complaint in the same format, "Oh, yes, this is a wonderful govment, wonderful." He then attacks the "mulatter," a "free nigger" from Ohio, a college professor, who had a shiny hat and white shirt: "And that ain't the wust. They said he could *vote,* when he was at home." Pap was about to vote "if I warn't too drunk to get there," but the idea of the "nigger" voting caused him to draw out of the 'lection. Pap's clothing, as described on his first appearance, is exactly the opposite of that of the black man. Educationally, as well, the two are polar opposites, one a professor, the other an illiterate who threatens and disrupts education. Pap raves on, attacking the government for not selling the infernal, thieving, "white-shirted free nigger." The obvious irony of the word "free" in this context assures us of Pap's bigotry.

The speech is Twain's most telling indictment of the corrupt interests that invest themselves in the support of any government; it stands as his comment on the selfishness that corrupts humanity in political power. The widow calling the "niggers" in for prayers, that first falsely casual reference, has provided Pap with the stage on which his present diatribe fits comfortably. Edgar Lee Masters criticized this speech because it did not go far enough in attacking government corruption, but the 1845 setting hardly allows Pap to go further; comments too directly oriented to the failure of civil rights action would have been as anachronistic as the Connecticut Yankee's telephones in Arthurian England. Instead, Twain provides immediate burlesque retribution for Pap's distortions by having him kick a washtub with his toeless boot. Degraded again, he rolls in the dirt, outswearing one of the region's greatest swearers. Such quick poetic justice is now Pap's pattern of life. The brief deadpan lines about Sowberry Hagan show Pap as a representative of his milieu. Huck has already remarked that Pap's barrel kicking "warn't good judgement"; his second comment that Pap's self-praise was "piling it on, maybe," finishes the identification of Huck as the passive but, again, dispassionate evaluator. Huck's detachment deflates the action for a moment, so Twain begins building Pap's expanded "two drunks and one delirium tremens" to complete the action begun at the judge's house. Pap's relationship with Huck, and Huck's own relationship with St. Petersburg, will climax in the most threatening violence so far in the novel.

J. T. Trowbridge's *Cudjo's Cave* (Boston: J. E. Tilton and Company, 1864) offers a passage remarkably close to Twain's depiction of Pap. Twain's use of the borrowed material is echoic rather than literal. The scene strengthens our sense of how Twain was drawing materials out of his own experience of America concerning the issues of slavery and individual rights. *Cudjo's Cave* is a Civil War novel treating the events of the early rebellion in Tennessee. As melodramatic as Twain's writing, it features hairbreadth escapes from death, near whippings of Negroes, and the ironic whipping of the villain's mother by the villain in a mistake, a death by drowning, and the rescue of a white by two blacks who appear to him as good and evil angels arguing over his survival in a dream. All events are punctuated by moral reasoning on right and wrong and freedom and slavery, and since one or two of the comments that Trowbridge puts in the mouths of his characters bear on *Huck Finn*, they will be mentioned in their place. The action here revolves around the attempt by drunken rebels to punish a blind Union minister by ransacking his house, burning his woodpile, and whipping his elderly freedman Toby. Their leader Silas Ropes gives a speech:

> "Free niggers is a nuisance," added Ropes, now very drunk, and very much inclined to make a speech on a barrel. . . "A nuisance!" he repeated with a hiccough, steadying himself on his rostrum . . . "And let me say to you, feller-patriots, that one of the glorious fruits of secession is, that every free nigger in the state will either be sold

for a slave, or druv out, or hung up. I tell you gentlemen, we're a goin' to have our way in these matters, spite of all the ministers in creation!". . .

"Who is boss here? Who ye goin' to mind? that old traitor, or me? I say, lick the nigger! We're a goin' to have our way now, and we're a goin' to have our way to the end of the 'arth, sure as I am a gentleman standing on this yer barrel!"

To emphasize his declaration, he stamped his foot; the head of the cask flew in, and down went orator, cask, and all, in a fashion rendered all the more ridiculous by the climax of oratory it illustrated. . .

Luckily, Silas had fallen partly in the barrel, and partly across the sharp edge of it, and being too tipsy to help himself, had been seriously hurt, and was now helpless. (105–7)

For Trowbridge in 1864, as for Twain in 1885, the same comic retribution follows the same drunken perversion of talk of rights in relation to "free niggers." The ellipses in the above passage represent moralistic speeches by the minister. For Twain, the issue is contained in the same terms but is further dramatized and individualized through its isolated location in Pap's cabin, when it poses a direct personal threat to Huck. Thus, the same materials that served Trowbridge in his general plot development serve Twain in the threatening private experiences observed by the hero, and soon to be burned further into his own psychology by Pap's attempt to kill him, ending with Huck barricaded behind Pap's turnip barrel.

The melodrama of Pap's degradation is completed after supper when he gets drunk, calls Huck the "Angel of Death," and then tries to kill him with a clasp knife. An elaborate and threatening chase scene develops, with Huck nearly being murdered. The dead are described as marching, snakes crawl up the legs of the screaming drunkard, and Pap "down on all fours"—grovelling humanity at its nadir—pleads with the dead to let a "poor devil" alone. Finally, with his terrifying "screechy" laugh and roar and cussing, he falls asleep, while saying to Huck he "would rest a minute and kill me." No more hellish indictment could be offered of a degraded "man" in the eyes of the reformers seeking to protect children from evil. And so the novel indicts vice through a picture to be shunned. Realism without authorial condemnation accounts for the mixed reception by adult critics of this portrait in a boy's book. Huck, protecting himself with Pap's own gun, is driven to the greatest extreme of potential violence we will ever see in him, here out of sheer self defense.

In the following chapter, Huck completes his plan to flee and Pap disappears from the novel until Jim's revelation of his death on the last page. Pap has served a major and crucial function, foreshadowing the perversions of political and social humanity which are elaborated in longer adventures in the novel. First, with his "call this a govment" speech he has accomplished a twofold purpose. He identifies the issue of the freedom of "niggers" as one which he as an evil and selfish man responds to with violence. He links his position to an ambiguity in government, tied to democracy but limited in action. Second, with his talk of rights and his stealthy returns by river, one more of which occurs in the following chapter, he establishes threatening resonances around villains rowing after Huck; this feeling will be expanded when the Duke and the Dauphin overtake the raft for the last time after the Wilks episode. Third, he is linked with Miss Watson as a repressive force threatening and dominating Huck Finn's freedom; although Huck's life in the cabin is dirtier and less verbally restrained, it is also lonesome and physically more dangerous. Pap and the widow and Thatcher resort to law and lawyers, and are all thus linked by their "sivilized" battles over Huck's wealth and life. As Huck announces his plans for escape to the reader, in the following chapter, he discloses his intention "to fix up some way to keep pap and the widow from trying to follow me." In this world, they are united.

The melodrama of the Angel of Death sequence is a violently shocking attempted murder—fully as squalid as any realistic pictures before seen in American literature. Pap's failure to reform his drinking, while defrauding the new judge and retaining custody of Huck, further implicates religious reformers of complicity in his violence. By chapter 8, the religious town and the drunkenly violent political outcast have been arrayed against Huck's individual interest. His deadpan narration of events, without protest, has identified him as a "naif," an innocent victim of their world—and he will free himself by covert actions rather than by open protest, the source and the significance of his seemingly chronic and sometimes seemingly purposeless lying.

Chapter 7 completes the introductory section which identifies Pap (govment) and Miss Watson and the widow (religion) as allied forces. Tom is a third force (representing learned authority), and both government and religion are based on that force. Huck has been presented as opposed to authority, without ancestors that benefit him; although

Pap threatens his life, he was not useful enough to get him into Tom Sawyer's gang. Although Miss Watson lectures and the widow praises him, they cannot ultimately give him personal release or defend him from Pap's malevolence. Introduced into the action have been the concepts of "free niggers," salvation and damnation—the two providences—and the conflicts of authorities, the burlesque of romantic sources, Huck's sense of himself as pragmatic in response to biblical teaching, and death and loneliness as Huck's great fears. Neither the town nor the river as setting has been particularly clearly depicted at this point in the novel, but Huck has looked over the Mississippi and seen it at night as "still and grand" and has identified town life as "cramped up and smothery." By the end of chapter 7, Twain the artist has foreshadowed every important point to come, nothing has been overlooked, including Huck's probable redeemability as commented on by the widow.

Even more important, the hell that Huck fears has been fully created within the emotional recognition of Twain's readers: a far darker hell than some critics presume. Marked at the beginning by Jim's light and dark angels and at the end by the Angel of Death, the Pap Finn sequence introduces the sense of darkness, hatred, imprisonment, and brutality that provide the emotional overtones for Huck's fears later in the novel's action. Critics who point out that Miss Watson's hell is not taken very seriously by Huck are correct only in terms of Huck's literal statements. Beyond this literal information lies the real power of fiction to create a rounded whole impression in place of a flat projection. The angels surrounding Pap are overt symbols of the force with which the first seven chapters define the milieu from which Huck flees as a compound of failed democracy and failed religion which threatens his life, safety, and peace. Even Twain in persona joked on the lecture platform that some people said heaven was a place where you went on learning and improving all the time, and that was his idea of hell. Twain as a novelist counts on the levelling of Pap and the townspeople through legal battles, through juxtaposition, and through veiled implications in such symbols as the angels and the marching dead in Pap's delirium to color our emotional response to Huck's thinking. Pap provides us with as scary a picture of hell as we will need to share Huck's fear at violating the social codes relating to "niggers," as defined preeminently by Pap. It is Pap's hell empowering Miss Watson's hell that Huck fears, a far more potent hell than most readers would have imagined or connected to "nigger-stealing" on their own.

– 5 –

Huck Acts, an Escape from Sivilization

Huck is a passive hero for most of the book. The negative description of his mother, his isolation and loneliness, and his laconic deadpan, self-effacing manner of humorous speech all seem to account for this passivity. Nevertheless, he reacts on Jim's behalf on several occasions in important ways. Unfortunately, the last part of the novel is dominated by twelve chapters in which Huck seems to do little in contravening the travesties worked by Tom Sawyer. The events of chapter 7 are crucial in establishing Huck's other side—his ability to act with determination. As readers who recognize this ability, we are prepared to find the last fifth of the novel especially frustrating.

Huck is aroused by his father after a night of terror, and offers a self-protective lie to escape further violence. We see our first extended view of the Mississippi River as Huck finds and hides a drifting canoe to use once he can "fix up some way to keep pap and the widow" from following him. Pap's "style," by no means as elaborate as Tom's but equally compelling, causes him to rush off to town for a drinking spree while Huck formulates and executes a brilliant plan to evade discovery; he loots the cabin, makes a false trail, and kills a wild pig and uses its blood to suggest that he was murdered and dumped in the river. The detailing here presents Twain at his best as an arresting realist. Dialect is primarily found in verbs, otherwise the short sentences and clear actions are straightforward. Huck remains detailed in his description, giving readers their second real taste of the Mississippi as he glides down it in his canoe, toward Jackson's Island, "dark and solid, like a steamboat without any lights."

Critics, like Bridges of *Life* in 1885, found the murder of a pig and the false murder unprepossessing. For Huck, however, it is his most dynamic act, fathered by the need for preservation; the sequence is inventive, well adapted to its milieu, and full of suspense. But it also has a special importance to the final outcome of the novel. As Huck proceeds, act by act, to create the perfect murder, he establishes his capacity for successful innovation, for carrying out complex life-saving projects. In short, he proves his abilities in contriving everything he might need to contrive at the end of the novel to secure Jim's escape from the Phelps Farm. This fact is the chief source of the tension we as readers feel at the end of the novel when Huck makes himself subservient to Tom's lesser travesty. So significantly less pointed are Huck's actions at the end of the book than here in chapter 8 that it has caused even the most sophisticated critics to assume that Twain merely fell into his ending. In fact, again in reversal, the ending is foreshadowed here; Twain establishes the basis for our frustration with and rejection of Tom's romantic shenanigans with Huck's coolly deliberate step-by-step execution.

If further evidence were needed to suggest how much the contrast between chapter 8 and the last twelve chapters of the book is designed to frustrate us as readers and heighten our disapproval of Tom's actions, Twain has provided the first evidence of a crucial motif following this plan. At the climax of his scheme, Huck declares: "I did wish Tom Sawyer was there, I knowed he would take an interest in this kind of business, and throw in the fancy touches." He adds a further line—"Nobody could spread himself like Tom Sawyer in such a thing as that"—to lead the reader away from a possible demurral; it was Tom who talked Huck back into town, and into his troubles with Pap and the widow. The second comment causes the reader to focus attention elsewhere. Huck's faked murder has a deeper undertone than Tom's apparent death by drowning in *Tom Sawyer*. Each time Huck refers to Tom's style in the future it will cause him trouble, and it will reemphasize the divergence of the two boys in their relation to reality.

The concluding paragraphs of the chapter treat us to Huck's first compelling descriptions of the starry night over the river, its sounds, and its beauty. The reader's real voyage of discovery is thus set to begin. Huck's ability to act decisively has been clearly demonstrated; it will be contrasted only later by his subservience and passivity in the face of Tom's more elaborate "style."

Huck's escape from Pap and "sivilization" initiates his meeting and joining with Jim on Jackson's Island. The Jackson Island interlude establishes trust between the two fugitives in an almost legalistic form. They begin to create a world and an ethic which will distinguish their raft on the Mississippi as one of the great American images of freedom and brotherhood. Tom Sawyer had also gone to Jackson's Island, in fact, and left the people on shore as sure of his death as they now are of Huck's. In the sentence-by-sentence texture of Huck's observations and objectives, however, tremendous differences can be discovered between his persona and Tom's. As the reader is initiated into the raft journey, he is also almost immediately intiated into Huck and Jim's more caring relationship, and sees Huck as a deeper mentality than Tom with simpler and more immediate concerns of food, safety, and survival. Because of Huck's dry humor and because of the more compelling results of his actions in regard to Jim, Huck is both detached from others and involved with them. His detachment is far more adult and Twainian than was Tom Sawyer's. Huck's closeness in mutual simplicity and sympathy with Jim provides him with his personal basis for abandoning the restrictions of the authorities of the village, their laws, and their public opinion.

Jackson's Island is first seen in the night, "big and dark and solid, like a steamboat without any lights." A big lumber raft is also seen coming, and Huck hears the voices of the men, one of Twain's many suggestions of heightened powers of perception on the river. After Huck naps, he wakes "in the grass and cool shade, thinking about things and feeling rested and rather comfortable": this is only the second time in the novel that he has registered "comfort." With "friendly" squirrels overhead, and feeling "powerful lazy and comfortable," Huck has attained the real boy's ideal state as identified in the literature of the realistic bad boys of the post–Civil War era.

In Tom Sawyer's Jackson's Island adventures (chapter 16 in *The Adventures of Tom Sawyer*) the natural observation is drawn out into an extended study of an inchworm that then gives way to boys swimming, and, finally, to a distant steamboat firing a cannon to raise the presumably drowned boys. In the following chapter, Tom visits his bereaved family, but does not take pity on them by revealing his survival, leaving that—with obvious cruelty—for a later grand entrance.

With Huck, events are much more tightly directed. Here, too, a steamboat floats on the river firing blasts to raise the presumably dead boy. But here, the people of the town form a unit on the steamboat. Huck "bosses" his own world, and ironically receives a "gift" by finding his daily bread. In the second paragraph, the cannon is already firing, as Huck explains with deadpan humor, "You see, they was firing cannon over the water, trying to make my carcass come to the top." Huck gets baker's bread, "what the quality eat," by fishing out a loaf in search of his "remainders." He comments that prayers that the bread find him must indeed work but "I reckon it don't work for only just the right kind," couching his disclaimer in countrified vernacular-sounding speech. Huck maintains the motif of concern over "the quality" and the right kind versus himself. His view of the steamboat is substantially closer than in *Tom Sawyer*; on the decks of "the ferry-boat full of people" he sees "Most everybody . . . Pap, and Judge Thatcher, and Bessie Thatcher, and Jo Harper, and Tom Sawyer, and his old Aunt Polly, and Sid, and Mary, and plenty more. Everybody was talking about the murder." Simultaneously, he is almost murdered in a comic moment when the Captain "hopes" Huck's body is washed ashore and Huck responds, "I didn't hope so," and a cannon blast then deafens Huck, "If they'd a had some bullets in, I reckon they'd got the corpse they was after." For Huck, the townspeople are a matter of closer but more detached detail than for Tom—and as he enumerates them name by name, the reader derives a sense of St. Petersburg's caste and class. For Huck, the ongoing deadliness is continuous and always surprising, although, as in the violence of a Buster Keaton film, not deadly. It will become deadly to Huck only through friends like Buck (rhymes with Huck) who is indeed found dead in the river. The action, for now, is wrapped in the deadpan voice of the comedian, dry detachment in keeping with his social detachment. But his humorous involvement has the implications of deadliness; on one side stand the townspeople on the steamboat, on the other the self-isolated practical boy, seeking merely his own comfort, safety, and survival—goals that the cast of characters on the boat would deny him.

Setting up housekeeping on the island, Huck occupies himself first with a businesslike examination of his island. Becoming "boss" of the island in a rather professional way, discovering both snakes, which will soon figure in the action, and the still-smoking ashes of a campfire, he is driven up a tree, out in a canoe, and finally into stealthy woodcraft and sophisticated detective work. Jim and Huck are quickly united at this point, for the ashes turn out to be Jim's fire, at which he is discovered sleeping the next night. Huck is, once again, taken for a dead person. But finally recognized as a live one, he enters into partnership with Jim. Huck and Jim establish at once the motif of mutual trust. Huck feels certain that he can count on *him* (Twain putting the pronoun for Jim in italics) not to tell. The sense of security in flight first goes Huck's way in this novel, since both Huck and Jim came to the island three days previously, shortly after Huck was killed, as Twain has Huck say it, using their easy literality to create verbal humor. They share a meal and comfort before Jim offers his confidence, in turn, to Huck.

Jim almost immediately, but with some caution, relies on Huck as deeply as Huck has relied on him. When Jim says that he *run off* (Twain again using italics, now for Jim's secret), it is couched amidst promises extracted from Huck not to tell. Huck even adds the proper ambivalence to his not telling by saying that people would call him a "low down Ablitionist and despise me," but he isn't going back there anyway—an early but clear statement that leaving a social setting frees the frontiersman from its flawed social beliefs and hatred of nonconformists. Yet Huck has been shown to have at first blush the continuing conscience of his community—as expressed earlier in Miss Watson's holding slaves and Pap's attitude toward "free niggers." For Huck and Jim, reciprocity is established in this initial interchange. Both are involved in life and death flights. Huck's defining battle later will be to retain his focus directly on the personalized ethic—his heart—which overcomes abstract ideas such as those which govern his antagonists.

Jackson's Island is still a place of nature as it was in *Adventures of Tom Sawyer,* but its quality is now joined to the problem of Huck's survival, Jim's freedom, and social ostracism. Tom observed an inchworm and went on playing; when Jim observes the birds flying low and predicts rain, he and Huck superstitiously move to higher ground, are saved from the rising river, and end up enjoying hot cornbread in their cave, secure above the flood. Huck's description of the thunderstorm includes metaphors of hell in references to "dark as sin" and "the underside of the world." For Huck and Jim, their folk superstition has saved them where religiosity would have been useless. This position contrary to Miss Watson's is developed through Twain's use of natural images and occurrences.

When Huck and Jim discuss bees not stinging idiots, Huck delivers his minstrel tag-line: "Jim said bees wouldn't sting idiots; but I didn't believe that, because I had tried them lots of times myself, and they wouldn't sting me." Nature in *Huck Finn* is part of the comic growth of the action—here Huck is the false-naif pretending to be a real naif. The effect of the minstrel format is to level both characters, uniting them in repartee, but allowing them the freedom of open discussion. In later minstrel sequences their open arguments reveal their presuppositions about mankind while pointing up their innocent virtue. The conversation here turns to livestock, a minstrel version of a bank swindle and, finally, for Jim's last ten cents, to Balum's Ass, who lost Jim's money, in a low-comedy repetition of Miss Watson's doctrine of gifts, by giving it to the poor at church. Burlesque nonsense though this seems, Twain the comic writer is still developing central issues. The ongoing considerations of how good is achieved, whether through religious or personal acts, is reviewed in caricature. These events lead Jim to reflect on slavery and the expropriation of a human being's value: "I owns myself, en I's wuth eight hund'd dollars. I wisht I had de money, I wouldn't want no mo'." Jim's reference to his value as a slave foreshadows his urge to buy his wife and children out of slavery. Thus, even silliness on Jackson's Island leads inevitably back into Huck and Jim's personalities, their safety, and the crucial social issues surrounding their lives. Snakes and practical jokes add further dimensions. The island *would* have to be "big and solid" to support this heavy a freight of the novel's developing themes.

Most of the island chapters are occupied with a rise in the river, punctuated with the "stock" minstrel routine. Huck and Jim also investigate a derelict house floating downstream, where Jim discovers a dead man but does not tell either Huck or the reader that it is Huck's father. Huck and Jim acquire a number of comic items, like a wooden leg ("we couldn't find the other one"), but the action is sinister, carried out in a devastated house with the "ignorantist" kind of words scrawled on the walls, and a dead body, shot in the back. They talk of riches and death and superstition. Knowledge of nature helps them to find comfort.

Huck's forgetfulness of natural rules causes him to nearly kill Jim when he attempts to play his first joke on Jim by curling a snakeskin in Jim's blankets. Huck's "ever so natural" joke is almost deadly as the snake's mate strikes Jim. The snake skin is a Tom Sawyer practical joke, but is significantly milder than the later stories of Bricksville loafers who like to set stray dogs on fire or tie tin pans to their tails to see them run themselves to death. In part, harsh-seeming practical jokes are part of Twain's realism, for country-style practical jokes are sometimes cruel beyond what contemporary urban-dwellers could imagine; earlier regional humorists—not only those of the Southwest—recorded many in their writings. However, hiding a snakeskin in Jim's blankets to frighten him is also, at the literary level, an example of the pattern of Tom going from play and more personal action to "effects" on other people, such as his aunt or the schoolmaster. When Huck attempts the same pattern, Jim is reduced to pulling on Pap's jug and declines into near-convulsions and death. His recovery takes four days and nights. Notably, Jim gets out of his head like Pap, and Pap is named and included in the resultant events, thus recalling as a consequence the novel's ugliest and most degraded scene. Since this action was Huck's, "all my fault," his embarrassment is an appropriate outcome—one which Twain will build on as Huck and Jim progress on the raft after the storm. After this first practical joke, Huck will make one more before abandoning such effects. Reasonably enough, the joke episodes are taken by most critics as crucial stages in Huck's maturation, and their use to show Huck's changing respect for Jim is clear evidence of how events are packed in the narrative, giving it a far more dramatic emotional development than occurs in *Tom Sawyer*.

Twain in this area of the book is establishing the character of his hero and the innocence with which he responds to the world. Huck on Jackson's Island shows special values. One close parallel example is J. T. Trowbridge's "Young Joe," the lead story in *Young Joe and Other Boys* (Boston: Lee & Shepard, 1879). It describes the adventures of an uneducated boy who takes a wealthy, somewhat vain, city baker on a duck hunt. The boy laughs at the errors of the poor-shooting greenhorn, and, when the greenhorn allows their dory to drift away, he must preserve them both on a storm-harried island by his ability to fish, hunt, and cook. In country dialect, the boy at first berates and goads the merchant, but soon laughingly accepts the situation, although still treating the merchant wryly and almost disdainfully. After Joe recovers the dory on the far side of the island, he allows the merchant to start unbuttoning his clothing to make flags to bring help, but stops him before the Nor'easter freezes him. He explains his prank by noting that the merchant went to sleep not thirty minutes after their first dinner, when work needed to be done to secure their survival. The merchant rewards the rough lad with his fine fowling gun, causing tears of gratitude in the lad's eyes, and achieving a sentimental completion. Without the melodrama of the murderous Pap, the story, even with its survival element, is less compelling. Jim's freedom also elevates the quest of Huck's story to a higher level as an American epic using American types. After all, Young Joe, as a country boy, is as American as Huck. But Twain has used the fictional medium with greater dexterity, making his hero more reticent, enlarging the nature and meaning of the action by reference to a great national issue. In comparing the voices of the two boy speakers, we see that Huck's is the more sympathetic, adult, humorous—both as naif and as dead-pan narrator. Twain's "softenings" of Huck make him the more potent narrator. "Young Joe" would repay further study by anyone seeking to determine the full extent of Huck Finn's uniqueness.

The minstrel routines also give evidence of how Twain builds motifs of importance using contemporary American materials and modes. Even in bits of narrative, the comedy of the naif is dominant. As Jim recovers from snakebite, Huck describes other examples of bad luck, including Old Hank Bunker, who looked at the moon over his left shoulder, got drunk, fell off the shot tower, and "spread himself out so that he was just a kind of layer, as you may say; and they slid him edgeways between two barn doors for a coffin. . . , but I didn't see it. Pap told me." The comic set-piece was a Twain favorite, appearing in his lectures and in *Roughing It,* after he converted it from stories heard elsewhere—one paradigm appearing in the *Yankee Blade* around 1847.[11] Here, it belongs to Huck not as a true story, but rather as a literalism borrowed from Pap, identified as an unreliable source. Huck is thus further matured as he borrows freely from a well-honed comic tradition of Yankee humor as converted by Mark Twain to western tall tales—a truly national blending. Huck's persona blends here with Twain's as lecturer, and he becomes the American literary comedian. Add to this persona the quest for freedom and safety on one of America's great arteries, and we do indeed have the stuff of a national epic.

Huck and Jim's next escape from trouble occurs when Huck, in girl's disguise, visits Mrs. Judith Loftus. Mrs. Loftus provides the second endorsement of Huck, following the widow's cautious approval early on. Again, the similarity to *Tom Sawyer* is notable, for Tom also left the island and went to shore to overhear the grief-stricken conversation of Aunt Polly, Sid, Mary, and Mrs. Harper, only to return with childish drama to reclaim a treasured chalk, rubber ball, and marble from his friends back at the hidden camp. Twain's invigorated and visionary sense of the melodrama of survival causes a heightened parallel by making the stakes of Huck's secret trip to shore the danger of discovery and capture by armed adults.

Mrs. Loftus is a gossipy newcomer whom Huck pumps for information. She speaks in another variant of Pike dialect about how much better off her relatives "used to was." She also reasons shrewdly about Jim, Pap, and the reward to be gotten by searching Jackson's Island. Huck, already at risk, becomes uncomfortable at the news of a greater threat. When Huck, uncharacteristically fidgeting, picks up a needle and threads it by poking the needle eye at the thread, Mrs. Loftus suspects and soon proves by several tests that he is a boy in disguise. A note on Twain's "realism" is in order here, since the needle-threading is sometimes pointed out as evidence of close attention to detail: in *The Prince and the Pauper* (chapter 13) Twain identifies the man's and woman's ways of threading needles as exactly opposite those ways described here; Twain was interested in realistic-seeming rather than accurate details—his is the art of comic plausibility, with the sex differentiation a symbolic point rather than a fact. It is at once as meaningful as all the other seemingly realistic details in the book, including the calling of Jim a "nigger." Incidentally, Mrs. Loftus calls Huck in disguise an "innocent" for not recognizing the importance of the three-hundred-dollar reward for Jim. She is thus attached to the world of money that Huck has fled. The money motif will be ongoing in relation to Jim's story, even to Jim himself.

Huck's fidgeting is hardly typical of his coolness in more difficult situations. When Mrs. Loftus discovers him to be a boy, she leaps to the assumption that he has been "treated bad"—which is true—and is a "runaway prentice"—which is not true. The business of discovery is elaborate, and at the point of confrontation, Mrs. Loftus looks at Huck "very pleasant. . . . I ain't going to hurt you, and I ain't going to tell on you, nuther." She uses the same currency of not telling as do Huck and Jim, and she concludes to protect "George Peters" and his "secret" . . . "treated bad. . . . Bless you child, I wouldn't tell on you." Her blessing foreshadows the more expansive offer to pray for him by Mary Jane Wilks later in the novel. The episode has three functions. First, it is part of a chain leading from the kindly Providence of the widow to the endorsement of Huck in the Wilks episode. Second, it advances the melodramatic action of disguise and escape that bears directly on the safety of Huck and Jim. Both are now clearly in flight from the slavery and repression attendant to their respective social levels. Behind them and behind this scene as motivation lies banishment down the river for Jim and loneliness and a possibly murderous imprisonment in an isolated cabin for Huck. Last, even the obviously kindly Judith Loftus is motivated by greed to recapture the runaway slave—but not the runaway apprentice—showing the corrupting influence of race even on this good person.

Biblically, Huck claims to be seeking Goshen rather than St. Petersburg as he develops a new lie to fit Mrs. Loftus's apprenticeship proposal. She gives him food and this time lets him escape. His departure occurs only after she questions him on his farm knowledge—more "stock" questions consistent with the Jackson Island discussion. She accepts the answers, but coaches him on how to disguise himself further and stands pat on her own decision to befriend the runaway white apprentice even while hoping to reap the reward from capturing the runaway black slave. Her skepticism shows in her naming of him: "Now trot along to your uncle, Sarah Mary Williams George Elexander Peters, and if you get into trouble you send word to Mrs. Judith Loftus, which is me, and I'll do what I can to get you out of it." She continues with words that would make a perfectly logical slave song if set to music: "Keep the river road, all the way, and next time you tramp, take shoes and socks with you. The river road's a rocky one, and your feet'll be in a condition when you get to Goshen, I reckon."

Huck's visit with Mrs. Loftus establishes a world distinct from the awful towns and plantations which Huck will visit. In this world, simplistic and folksy, kindliness and knowledge are distinct from social standing and from established social connections. Mrs. Loftus is both a newcomer to the community and an insightful humanitarian—the sort who might see "youth" in a full-grown humorist, for example, as did Livy with Clemens. Economics governs attitudes toward Jim, and knowledge of who murdered Huck—Jim or Pap—is hidden in ignorance and supposition, but greed dominates. The episode embodies Twain's mentality as a comic spokesman for the new American frontier, with the ethical ambiguity of changing social relationships and the powerful humanity of free men let loose to make their own way in the world. The episode is yet another appropriate entryway for an American epic, reflecting American experience as personalized in Twain's own life and now converted into the imagery and language of his comic fiction.

Huck, of course, has his own set of hidden allegiances, developed in the previous episodes, to Jim, and so uses all his skills to secure Jim's escape, carefully noting times, doubling back, and lighting a decoy campfire to throw off pursuit. Huck quickly arouses Jim: "Git up and hump yourself, Jim! There ain't a minute to lose. They're after us!" This use of the word "us" represents the full joining of the fates of the two refugees: "Jim never asked no questions, he never said a word; but the way he worked for the next half an hour showed about how he was scared. By that time everything we had in the world was on our raft. . . ." Without lights, "dead still, without saying a word," Huck and Jim on the raft slip below the tip of Jackson's Island—and—in silence and darkness, without any fanfare of false "style"—begin the greatest literary voyage in later nineteenth-century fiction.

– 6 –

The Raft and the River:
Defining an Ethic

The chapters comprising Huck and Jim's initial raft voyage down the Mississippi are crucial to the shaping of Twain's positive vision and, along with important expansions of our understanding of the significance of the raft in chapter 19, they establish the philosophy that endows the power of the river with the undertow of humanity. Huck and Jim come to a higher level of relationship which is the basis for Huck's final powerful decision to go to hell. Even as Huck and Jim slide below the tip of Jackson's Island, Huck says that his tricky campfire "played it as low-down on them as I could," revealing his ambivalence about helping Jim. When Huck plays tricks on Jim and is reprimanded, he and Jim together create a better practical ethic than others provided them by American society, thus continuing the pattern of rejecting the ethics of the small town represented by Miss Watson and Pap. In the colorful description of the Mississippi flatboatmen, so long excised from the standard texts, Huck is shown further kindness as a "cub." The raft world allows for a finer ethic, formed in the natural background of "the big river," which Huck and Jim develop for themselves as they discuss pragmatism, kings, and right treatment versus trash-like treatment of friends.

Twain maintains excitement through descriptive details interwoven with philosophic discussions such as the one concerning "borrowing." Local details of the river foreshadow the raftsmen chapter, as even a "tow-head" is carefully described—with vernacular phrases—as "a sand-bar that has cotton-woods on it as thick as harrow-teeth." Huck rejects Jim's gossipy reasoning about their escape from Mrs. Loftus's husband by saying that he doesn't care what the reason was that they weren't caught just so long as they weren't—a mode of expressing his tension as aptly restrained as in Hemingway's heroes. Jim also mentions that they would have been returned to "the same old town" again. The opposite state of their present life is thus defined at the outset of the voyage. In comparison, the building of a comfortable raft, with floor elevated above steamboat waves and a shelter for protection from rain and sun, is detailed. Even the rules of navigation for safety from steamboats are outlined, foreshadowing a dramatic moment to follow.

Most important is the formation of a special raft ethic, carefully and comically worked out by Huck and Jim. One of Twain's best humorous statements, it takes only three paragraphs to outline. First Huck recounts running eight hours at night, swimming, now and then, catching fish, "kind of solemn, drifting down the big still river," lying on their backs, talking and occasionally chuckling in low tones to each other. Even as they pass St. Louis with its thousands of twinkling lights, there is no sound—the river is a special place, a holy churchlike place—even as early as chapter 12.

The discussion revolves around being "comfortable" about "borrowing." Huck slipped ashore nights and sometimes lifted a chicken that wasn't roosting comfortable. In *Pudd'nhead Wilson,* Twain would excuse the slave who lured a cold chicken to step onto a warm board and into his bag; his action was part of the natural outcome of slavery. In caricature morality, Huck reports, "Pap always said, take a chicken when you get a chance, because if you don't want him yourself you can easy find somebody that does, and a good deed ain't ever forgot." As with the Hank Bunker story, Huck detaches himself from Pap's statement, but its terms are both comic and appropriate. The presumption is that the self-centeredness of the frontiersman on the ownerless frontier becomes ironic humor in the settled areas where chickens are owned. The attachment of good deeds to theft, and the finding of someone else who needs help, carries forward the terms in which Huck prayed and got a fishline. Continuing to reason, Huck offers the concept of "borrowing" things as interpreted by the widow—just stealing. Since Jim is to be developed as a level-headed "nigger," he is allowed the resolution of the conflict between authorities: "the widow was partly right and pap was partly right," and so Huck and Jim agree not to borrow unripe fruit—"because crabapples ain't ever good." Conflicts between authorities have set Huck and Jim free, and they accomodate themselves. Huck once again feels "comfortable," always a key word distinguishing freedom from authoritarian repression. Providing one more level of conflict between right and wrong, Twain develops his action through comedy toward the later climax—the crucial machinery of the novel is comic here, the achievement of Twain the deadpan ironic humorist.

A number of flamboyant elements dot chapters 12 through 19: the *Walter Scott* episode, reasoning on Sollermun and Frenchmen borrowed from a minstrel routine, the raftsmen chapter, Huck's first decision not to turn Jim in, the Grangerford-Shepherdson feud, and the entry of the Duke and Dauphin. The episodes are either reprises of the themes already developed or expansions of them pointing forward to even greater levels of spiritual development. The *Walter Scott* exemplifies Twain's method of compacting moral action within the comic irony of a melodramatic event—a method practiced in the character of Yokel and the robber gang in *The Prince and the Pauper* and in Morgan le Fay's dungeons in *A Connecticut Yankee* as well as in Huck's narrative.

As Huck and Jim get comfortable with their ethics about borrowing, they discover the sinking derelict steamboat *Walter Scott*. The use of the English romancer's name implicates southern romanticism, which Twain saw as a bankrupt tradition. She has "killed herself" on a rock and Jim is "dead against" landing. Huck forces the landing on the "mournful and lonesome" derelict by appeal to Tom Sawyer—recalling the essential feelings that Tom Sawyer engendered in Huck at the novel's opening, but altering their format. Huck might "borrow" something: seegars of the "rich" captain might be on board . . . the landing is to be an "adventure," "for pie," with "style," and a chance to "spread" out in Sawyer fashion. Motives that had caused Tom to endanger Huck in the original joke on Jim are thus represented to the reader in Huck's actions, but with a radically expanded melodrama. Pointing forward in the novel, they also foreshadow the last fifth of the book.

"Rights" are reintroduced now in a way which, following Pap's "call this a govment" speech, finishes undermining accepted political morality as a guide to action. Huck and Jim overhear two villains discuss plans to kill a third over his share of their thefts. Huck again invokes Tom Sawyer as a reason for not backing out of the now expanded danger of real thievery rather than Tom's imaginary robber exploits. The most important action relates to talk of "rights" and "morals," talk attaching Tom Sawyer's themes to Pap Finn's. The chief robber repeats and expands Pap's philosophy, including some of the same words and concepts, and in an identically spiteful and angry tone, plans a murder. The speech is directed to a third robber, bound and helpless, rather than to the unseen Huck: "Hear him beg! and yit if we hadn't got the best of him and tied him, he'd a killed us both. And what for? Jist for noth'n. Jist because we stood on our *rights*— that's what for." Reeking of whiskey to the breathless Huck, the robbers continue the discussion on the basis of "good sense" and "ways that's jist as good" to prevent "State's evidence" without bringing risks—the language of law as Pap used it. Jim Turner will be left to drown: "I'm unfavorable to killin' a man as long as you can git around it; it ain't good sense, it ain't good morals. Ain't I right?" Pap the murderous drunkard who perverts the language of law and morality is now expanded to a "gang of murderers," whose mere existence is bound up with the melodramatic crisis of the dying ship.

The completion of the event allows Twain to bring in Huck's own irony, as well. He restates the religious position of the widow and Miss Watson, thus finishing the progressive expansion of Huck's town life to a wider level of experience. Later, Tom Sawyer will become the ultimate generalizer of doing good to people who don't need it by freeing Jim when he is already free. As Huck realizes that he and Jim have escaped "safe" from the sinking boat and left the gang of murderers to perish, he worries about their dreadful fix, putting himself in their situation and accepting blame for their state with half-naive logic. He determines to "get them out of their scrape, so they can be hung when their time comes." (It is down in the bills, we remember, that Huck will be hung.) Huck later rues the punishment of human beings by others even more poignantly; here, his sympathy is consistent with the burlesque humanity by which he and Jim reason, putting life above law. Huck approaches a ferryboat captain and preys on his jealousy and opportunism towards "rich" Jim Hornbeck to convince the man he will be paid handsomely for going to the wreck to rescue the rapscallions. For the reader, in soliloquy, Huck then outlines his moral position as having fulfilled the nonsense aims of Miss Watson's morality, with all its profit only for others, and frequently—as in the attempt to reform Pap—for the unworthy:

> But take it all around, I was feeling ruther comfortable [note the
> word again], on accounts of taking all this trouble for that gang,
> for not many would a done it. I wished the widow knowed about
> it. I judged she would be proud of me for helping these rapscallions,
> because rapscallions and dead beats is the kind the widow and good
> people takes the most interest in. (91)

Huck's irony expresses Twain's own antagonism toward misdirected
charity. Few readers may sense this as literally Huck; it is Mark
Twain's voice, recapturing Huck's original findings in the woods outside St. Petersburg and preparing us for the ultimate expansion of
those findings in chapter 31. Huck must immediately shrug off the
death of the gang, as his plan fails; he comments coolly that if they
could stand it, he could.

Huck and Jim, now left briefly to themselves, engage in burlesque
discussions on King Solomon (Sollermun, to them) and Frenchmen.
Since they will be invaded by a fake king and duke, one of whom
claims to be the lost dauphin of France, both discussions are foreshad-
owings. Huck also tells the reader that he read to Jim of kings and
dukes and earls. Twain uses the discussions to make statements, in
burlesque, about valuing human life, thereby continuing the moral arguments of the book. In "Was Sollermun Wise," Jim rehashes with
Huck the idea of many wives making life noisier than a boiler factory,
with the factory having the advantage of being able to shut down.
Several literary comedians, including Artemus Ward and Max Adeler,
had used the same comic ideas in discussing Brigham Young and the
Mormons. The pointed part of the discussion comes when Jim complains that Sollermun's judgment, to divide a baby between the two
mothers who claimed it, was a result of his not valuing children because he had so many. Jim's own sensitivity to his children is thus
anticipated, and the intensity of Jim and Huck's respect for each other
is reflected.[12] A fool's argument, Jim's aggressively simplistic position
puts the survival of the baby above the devices of justice; this idea of
course, is a version of *Huck Finn*. Huck will make a similar decision.
And corresponding decisions have already been made by Judge
Thatcher and Mrs. Loftus. Unlike the Dickensian novelistic conventions, which allowed a character to flatly declare that the law's an ass,
Mark Twain uses the texture of a minstrel show interrogatory to reach
the same conclusion.

Jim and Huck's discussion of the French language presents similarly sophisticated ideology hidden beneath burnt cork minstrel dialect. It has the effect of leveling Huck and Jim, as Huck the wise pragmatist is baffled by Jim's apparently foolish arguments. Huck attempts to explain to Jim that Frenchmen talk in a different language than English and mentions the "dolphin," who some say came to America after "Louis Sixteenth" got his head cut off. Jim wonders if he can get a "situation," and what he can do without work, questions which Twain would later go on to elaborate in an entire novel, *The American Claimant*. As Huck tells Jim a French phrase, he explains that French and English are different just as cats and men talk differently. Jim counters that a cat is not a man and therefore has no need to talk like a man: "why doan he *talk* like a man!" Huck says, "you can't learn a nigger to argue. So I quit." At the opening of the same chapter, Huck had said that Jim had an uncommonly level head "for a nigger." Such a chapter challenges racial stereotypes by putting them forward so boldly that they become questionable. Two points of humanism are raised. The question of Huck's using "nigger" to dismiss Jim, shows up the use of the epithet as an *ad hominem* shift in logic—a cheap way out, as seen in earlier uses of the term. Also, the question of what is a man was asked by all the literary comedians and answered comically by defining a complex of decency and integrity.[13]

Under both routines is a current of refusal to accept surface conventions. Each routine is thus a paradigm of philosophical revisionism. Jim's literal logic accepts no "sivilized" analogy; the real Solomon's judgment is based on a manipulation of terror—only a detached person could employ it; the real standing of a man is based on universal kindness and attachment. Even Jim says that he would let a white man call him things that no "nigger" could—obviously aware of caste and class in the South. Motifs of child caring, royalty and immorality, and social hierarchy—which both Huck and Jim adhere to—are developed, along with a comic style of discussion that recurs when Tom Sawyer appears later at the Phelps Farm. Huck and Jim have been working out their own way of thinking, in humor and in travesty. They are now beginning to show their freedom from established authority and unquestioning obedience to official logic. Twain's humor, even when seeming undirected, advances the main motif of the novel.

Huck will undergo a significant development because of his second attempt to play a practical joke on Jim. Deluding Jim about witches, as Tom Sawyer had done in St. Petersburg, was shallower than this adult business. Here, Huck and Jim encounter fog, and Huck in the canoe becomes separated from Jim on the raft. Huck can only find his way back after a scary separation. For a time, the river itself is "monstrous big" with solid walls of formidable trees, but a frantic chase after black specks on the water finally brings Huck to the raft, where he finds Jim asleep with his head down between his knees, with one of the raft's oars smashed off, "So she'd had a rough time." Huck's response is to pretend to be just waking up, assigning the storm to Jim's nightmares, playing on Jim's imagination now as had Tom earlier.

Huck's joke triggers a vastly different response from the hair-ball routine and the witch-ride story earlier. The more intimate and caring relationship of Huck and Jim changes the outcome profoundly, as Jim looks at the trash on the raft and realizes that Huck has been playing a practical joke. Jim responds that when he found Huck, "de tears come en I could a got down on my knees en kiss' yo' foot I's so thankful. En all you wuz thinkin 'bout wuz how you could make a fool uv ole Jim wid a lie." Jim defines those who abuse their friends as "trash" and Huck, in turn, confesses that he could have gotten down on his knees and kissed Jim's foot: "It was fifteen minutes before I could work myself up to go and humble myself to a nigger—but I done it, and I warn't ever sorry for it afterwards." Twain's use of the term "nigger" is perhaps most potent here because, like the Samaritan in the Christian parable, it denotes the lowest and most despised. Since the term "trash" has a second possible implication in relation to the term "white trash," the suggestion of caste is pervasive. So Huck finds himself willing to lower himself for the sake of friendship and respect. Huck vows to do no more mean tricks, putting aside the exploitive part of his friendship with Jim and keeping the more adult, caring elements. The business related to Tom's candle theft and Jim's witch-ride is now rectified. Even more important, the central difference between the relationships on the raft and those on the shore has now been made explicit.

In manuscript, a long chapter describing the life of a flatboatman added local color to the front end of the river voyage and balanced chapters showing yokels at the end of the novel. Twain allowed the chapter to be deleted so that his publisher Charles Webster would have similarly sized volumes to sell as a set of Tom and Huck's adventures. Now restored in the California Edition of *Huck Finn,* the chapter adds several important effects. First, it gives an overview of characters on a flatboat, parallel, but lower in class and behavior, to the residents of St. Petersburg. Huck and Jim's isolated relationship is thus played out against an even larger panorama. Second, the reader receives a full introduction to the river type, moderating the effect of Pap, otherwise the only sample in the early part of the book of the common man. Since later samples abound, including Boggs and the yokels at the Phelps Farm, the flatboatmen chapter strengthens the symmetry of the book, develops the reader's sense of a world that features a full range of coarseness and ignorance to complement the violence and pride displayed through the Grangerfords and Colonel Sherburn among the quality, and increases our sense of the popular mind. The gullibility of the townspeople in the Wilks episode, the casual cruelty of the Bricksville loafers and the lack of control and behavior at the camp meeting are foreshadowed. Twain offers a rough-looking lot, drinking from a jug, and singing a song which "wasn't a nice song—not for a parlor anyway," thus establishing an alternative against which we may later measure Emmeline Grangerford's poetry, which *is* fit for a parlor.

The "monstrous long raft" is in itself as long as a procession—a word Twain uses in his sociopolitical description of Arthurian England in *A Connecticut Yankee*. With as many as thirty men, it carries five wigwams, suggestive of the political symbols of the Democratic party and Tammany Hall. Such an idea might be farfetched, but Twain goes on to describe the tall flagpole at each end of the raft, further suggesting that this is an American spectacle. So rough are the flatboatmen, indeed, that in true Davy Crockett and Mike Fink fashion, one—the "Child of Calamity"—boasts about his invincibility in fighting, calling himself the "copper-bellied corpse-maker from the wilds of Arkansaw." His opponent, too fiery to be viewed except through smoked glass, claims "the boundless vastness of the great American desert" as his property. Like Yankee boasters who saw their scope expanding from the equator to the aurora borealis, he claims to be a national figure who boils the Gulf of Mexico and drags the Atlantic for whales with a net made from the lines of longitude and latitude. The two are true representatives of the universal Yankee nation at its most grandiose, and unabashed propagators of the American frontier brag. In a variation on the old Sut Lovingood yarns, a small chap then beats up both men.

After a brief hoedown, the story of Dick Allbright and the

haunted barrel offers another version of the motif of child brutality and child murder, now as comic ghost story. A barrel containing the corpse of the dead baby Charles William Allbright haunts a raft and brings death to it in the manner of the Ancient Mariner. Twain uses this device to attach ghostly feelings to rafting, even though the story becomes comic almost at once. The yelling and jeering at the tale's teller, however, leads to the discovery of the naked and vulnerable Huck, hidden among the watermelons. At first he is threatened with being painted blue, but the boatman Davy takes pity on Huck who is "nothing but a cub." As in the Judith Loftus episode, Huck lies—How did you get so dry?/I'm always that way, mostly—but his lies are successful when he gives his own name as Charles William Allbright. The rough kindly men release Huck, and on his escape he enters into the first of his great soliloquies on the freeing of Jim and his own social standing. Set against the stories, threats, and, ultimately, sympathy from the flatboatmen, Huck's own mind seems reasonable both in its adherence to the group—for hooting is vented on the storyteller who is declared an outsider—and in his own kindliness—as just seen in Davy. The episode exemplifies symphonic repetition as it develops the book's central idea.

The episode offers both local color, stamping this as a portrait of life on the river, and establishes more definition of the class represented in its most corrupted form by Pap. The chapter paints the frontier in bright colors, full of the comic exaggeration attributed to the frontier as a unique American locale. In this respect, the chapter adds to the book's status as an American novel. However, thematic development is equally important. After Huck has been on the flatboat, the camp meeting fleeced by the Dauphin and in fact the Duke and Dauphin as characters themselves, are more clearly related to this world—they are the rough, frontier element, and their existence prevents us from thinking that the frontiersmen are different from others in this society; it is not only local color, it is Twainian literary realism.

The passage also helps Twain move Huck and Jim's raft past Cairo, Illinois, and the obvious entrance of the Ohio River, with its clear water, into the muddy Mississippi. We gain sufficient information from the raftsmen about the merging of the two rivers to understand the new difficulty in Huck and Jim's intended plan to canoe to freedom. Stories of murderers and tall tales show Huck's lies to be merely the currency of society, with the difference that his lies are directed toward preserving Jim's safety. Thus, as he leaves the flatboat and returns to Jim on the raft, the stage is set for an expansion of Huck's ambiguous sense of his relationship to Jim and a further development of Huck as defender of Jim despite the "conscience" imposed on him by Miss Watson's St. Petersburg.

As with Pap, Jim is affected by his family in a way that suggests the experience of a family man from Hartford, Connecticut. Sensing freedom, Jim reveals to Huck that he plans to buy or steal his wife, and then to buy or steal his two children. "Stealing" rather than "borrowing" causes Huck's "conscience," derived from Miss Watson, to upbraid him for not telling on Jim. He is miserable and wishes he was dead, displaying emotions originating with his village experience. As Huck paddles off to salve his conscience by telling on Jim, however, Jim calls after him that he's "the *only* fren' ole Jim's got now." Jim calls Huck his only "true" friend and the "on'y white genlman" that ever kept his "promise" to old Jim, referring to Miss Watson's promise not to sell him down the river and Huck's promise to keep his secret. In *Cudjo's Cave,* the worst of the secesh slavers also called themselves "gentlemen," and the term has a slight irony even as Jim uses it here. The moment allows Twain to change the terms of Huck's mental discussion from social expectations to personal relationships. Twain's ultimate political stance is individualistic. Placing all of his philosophical belief in the value of personal loyalty and humanity above codes, Twain next casts Huck's decision in terms of the South and his localist setting by challenging Huck through the device of two men seeking runaway slaves.

Hunters of escaped slaves dramatize Huck's new ideology, playing it against the inhumane profit motive. Slave hunters approach Huck and ask him if his "man" is white or black; Huck, "weakening" on Jim's behalf, convinces them that the raft is occupied by his smallpox-infected family. Huck rises above codes of color to codes of humanity. The hunters, in selfish fear, put two twenty-dollar gold pieces on a log and float them to Huck, coaching him about how to deceive others into helping his infected family and possibly suffer contagion. This is the first reference to a forty-dollar payment for Jim, and it derives from human meanness, as does the men's seemingly helpful advice to Huck on getting help lower down the river. The incident offers a harsher revision of the Judith Loftus incident. Huck's emotional turmoil here is as melodramatic as was his anxiety earlier about drowning on the *Walter Scott,* as the issue of loyalty between the races overcomes social boundaries. Twain intensifies Huck's natural response by externalizing the conflict through outsiders intruding upon Huck even as he himself reasons. Huck is challenged to overcome a sense of responsibilities to slavery in terms of people who have done him "no harm." Although the last conclusion is debatable in fact, its intensely moral terms are allied to the discussion of heaven and hell which has been going on since the beginning of the book. Huck has been harmed and maligned by this discussion, as much as his society's catchphrase, here used, maligns Jim: "Give a nigger an inch, and he'll take an ell," presented in quotations marks to designate it as the imposition of common social thought on Huck. Trowbridge's *Cudjo's Cave* (217–18) distributes such ambivalence among opposing characters, with one "bigoted and unforgiving" character contending, "Nothing under the sun shall make me give encouragement to a nigger's running away," while another Union slaveholder responds, "I can't say as I ever felt it was such a divine insitution as some try to make it out, and I don't believe there's a man here that thinks in his heart that it's just right. And as for the niggers running away, my private sentiment is, that I don't blame 'em a mite." Huck's sound heart helping Jim in the face of religious law is prefigured in this speech by Trowbridge's hero. Huck's naturalness derives form his truthfulness to this strand of thought in the portrayal of the American character.

Huck's final reasoning about saving Jim by lying to the men is a denial of conscience which is carefully developed by Twain. Huck mourns that he didn't get started right so it wasn't any use for him to try to learn to do right. Considering his upbringing with Pap, this might make some sense, although we have already seen the contrary training by the widow. However, the men who were hunting runaway slaves also had senses of guilt. When they refuse to help Huck's "small-pox" raft they accuse him of being willing to spread the disease all over, give him twenty-dollar gold-pieces as apology for not helping him, and then counsel him to go to a town further down and, "Don't be a fool again, and let people guess what is the matter. Now we're trying to do you a kindness; so you just put twenty miles between us." With these words, the men's "charity" is identified not only as selfish but as harmful to others. Nineteenth-century codes of virtue could hardly have named a more venal hypocrisy, but their position will be expressed at least once more in the novel by the youngest of the Wilks girls. When Huck declares that he'd feel even worse if he'd turned Jim in, it is obvious that he would have turned Jim over to men with little feeling for other men. Thus, there is considerable driving force behind his now-strengthened resolve, pointing him toward Miss Watson's hell: "what's the use you learning to do right, when it's troublesome to do right and ain't no trouble to do wrong, and the wages is just the same? . . . So I reckoned I wouldn't bother no more about it, but after this always do whichever come handiest at the time." Huck disguises his sentiments in a vulgarly offensive concern with profit—a low viewpoint consistent with the motif of bosses, situations, and profits throughout the book.

Huck's preference for doing what is handiest has already been defined by contrast with the pragmatism of the immoral slave-hunters; Huck, as we know from his remorse over the snakeskin and "trash" episodes, seeks good for others. So close is the framework of this experience to Huck's later resolve to work for Jim, that Huck has little further to go in his ethical decision to decide to go to hell. In fact, Twain sends just such an image to sink the raft. As Jim despairs that "Po' niggers can't have no luck," a steamboat with fiery teeth like glowworms runs over the raft amidst a pow-wow of cussing—images of the hell-bound train melodramatically displayed for the popular reader. Huck calls out for Jim but gets no response and swims ashore to be greeted by howling dogs. The raft world is suspended while other themes of culture, social reasoning, quality, and inhumanity are developed through the Shepherdson-Grangerford feud in the following chapters.

The Shepherdson-Grangerford feud comes at a particularly important time in the book. The crescendo of the massive steamboat crushing the raft thrusts the reader suddenly into a fully realized level of violence. Here the violence, differing from that associated with Pap's outcast status, is institutionalized: Colonel Grangerford is of the aristocracy. The widow Douglas and Pap would both agree on endorsing his high quality, and Huck accepts it, too, even as we the readers are induced by Twain's references back to the two earlier figures of St. Petersburg to see the colonel as the embodiment of their philosophy. They were merely townspeople. Colonel Grangerford is an aristocrat, with clothing and demeanor to match—Twain offers a syllogistic progression up the social ladder. Shortly after this episode, Twain will move us to the highest rung of his social progression, bringing forth a duke and the lost king of France.

Colonel Grangerford shares with his society a suppressed capacity for violence as frightening as Pap's overt brutality. From his eyes, light-nings flash, and his first response to "George Jackson" is to have George's pants patted down to check for concealed weapons. The world he presides over is openly murderous. Colonel Grangerford's family shows Twain's brilliant use of the episodic format to create a symphonic progression. Where Tom Sawyer's gang was manipulated by Tom's fatuous distortion of his "authorities," this family is ruled by a set of books that only Huck reads, and by poetry that is a travesty of the sentimental; its notion of art is Emmeline's spidery eight-armed weeping maidens and bowls of plaster fruit with chips showing their falseness. Even more impressive is that in both Tom's and Buck's case we have words defined that deal with criminal acts. Tom's word is "ransomed," which he defines as killing, although he never kills any-one. Buck's word is "feud," but now real murder *is* done, and the extended violence, under Huck's questioning, is revealed to have lost whatever motive it may once have had. It is now murder for the sake of revenge. The implications of Tom's perversion of ideas is carried into a deeper reality, building the tension of the novel. The fact that Huck cannot remember his own made-up name and depends on Buck to get it misspelled for him as George Jaxon has the force of implicat-ing Huck himself as part of the ignorance of his surroundings, and so Twain shows Huck partly compromised here as elsewhere by his al-legiance to this civilization.

Religion is developed similarly. From Miss Watson's mean-spirited view of Providence, the reader now comes to the Granger-fords' trip to church. They carry guns, which they set between their legs. Listening to the sermon on brotherly love, Huck feels the "or-neryness" of the moment and labels it as one of the roughest Sundays he ever experienced. The double irony of hogs going voluntarily to church offers comic relief from this tension. Notably, a hymn book becomes the agent of the escape of the two lovers, triggering the death of Buck and the complete breakdown of civil order, with bands of murderous men riding here and there along the darkening river bank.

Huck's consequent escape to the raft is one of the brightest mo-ments of the book: the moment which fixes and defines the meaning of the raft as a "home" for Huck and Jim. It is at the end of chapter 28 that Huck calls the raft "home": for the first time in the novel he has so located himself emotionally in the world. Although Jim's calling Huck "Honey" has been mischievously interpreted by Leslie Fiedler as a homosexual element, it is indeed a moment which displays the deep affection growing between Jim the adult slave and Huck the young white master, replacing the master-slave relationship. The next few pages describing the philosophy of the raft and the raft idyl are possibly the finest nature descriptions in American fiction, and they bring the humanity of the heroes to its finest realization, as they drift along outside of society and the influence of social artifacts.

The chapters on the Shepherdson-Grangerford feud offer a progression and expansion of the themes of the novel as already developed in the early chapters. They begin with a discussion of social quality and end with the murder of a young boy, much as the St. Petersburg chapters began with the training of Huck and ended with Pap attempting to kill him. But during this later sequence, Huck's fraudulent murder is reproduced, with melodramatic horror, with the real murder of Buck, the youngest Grangerford, Huck's friend.

The symphonic evolution of various cultural elements is notable here. It is emphasized by the newly added flatboatmen chapter through a variety of repetitions. In the first edition of 1885, the poetry of Emmeline Grangerford stands alone, but with the rough songs of the rivermen added in their chapter, her grotesquely sentimental offerings represent a segment of shore society corresponding to the society of the squalid flatboatmen. The songs of each represent their tawdry cultural life—one sexually indecent, the other bathetically morose and death-oriented, burlesqued in the later case by the gruesome comedy of Emmeline's pointedly comic race with the undertaker. The sequence is obviously a literary travesty with no pretense to real life, and so treated by the illustrator Kemble, who abandoned Huck in one illustration to illustrate one of Emmeline's poems. Both the flatboatmen and the Grangerfords are preoccupied with death, threatened by violence, and pretentiously proud. One is low on the social ladder, the other high; together they represent a complete milieu. Where the flatboatmen are openly violent and offer frontier boasts, the Grangerfords are restrained but offer the flashing looks of pride. They represent equivalent sides of a complete world, now symphonically elaborated.

As earlier, with the village folk on the steamboat, Huck is faced with an entire spectrum of the family, both gentle and proud, although here they do not actually fire guns as did the steamboat. In fact, Huck is easily welcomed into the family, once again sporting a false name and an invented life story. It could be that Huck deserves interpretation as a wily confidence man, but his purpose is not, in fact, to derive any benefit from the Grangerfords by cheating them. The welcome that might "take" his head off is ironic; there is an obvious falsity in the Grangerfords' socially respectful fashion of frisking Huck's pockets "from outside." Generously, they offer Huck a home. Moses and Solomon are reinvoked by Buck, who reechoes Biblical names by asking where Moses was when the lights went out. Huck this time, shifting easily into Jim's role, takes the literal position. This short-hand by Twain establishes the commonality between Huck, Buck, and Jim. Huck's feelings at the later loss of Buck will become part of our understanding of how he would "feel" if he were to betray Jim. Such a seemingly trivial moment—a lame joke—carries part of the underlying emotional business of the novel; Twain uses bad humor as purposefully as refined humor or irony.

The decor of the Grangerford house is the most carefully detailed in the book. Huck says he has never before seen a country house this "nice," with this much "style." Split-bottom chairs have no sag; "nice" and "big brass" fire irons establish the home as one of means. The details which Huck overtly admires caricature the plantation taste of the era before the war, with Emmeline Grangerford's poetry and pictures as the most grotesque elements. Ultimately, the artifacts also bring their own sets of associations to the novel; they suggest inefficiency, ineptness, and sloppy sentiment. The travesty of sentimentalized and cheapened popular romanticism also further undercuts the reliance by Tom Sawyer on the same sorts of romantic devices. Their style and Tom's have much in common, as Twain suggests by using the key word "style" to apply to both. One of the most obvious malfunctions of purpose is suggested by a comic bit common in domestic comedy of the period: the clock which ticked pleasingly and would strike a hundred and fifty times before she got tuckered out. Likewise, a chalkware fruit basket with colors gaudier than the real thing shows white chips; crockery dogs and cats squeak but don't open their mouths or look interested. Huck's observation is designed by Twain to be so literal that everything has flaws.

The cultural details are as exact as the aesthetic ones. The speeches of Clay identify the southern border-state locale, and the Bible, *Pilgrim's Progress,* and *Gunn's Family Medicine* are appropriate to the setting and define its level of culture. "Friendship's Offering" represents a genre of token giftbooks of the period, full of beautiful "stuff" and poetry. Huck claims to read Bunyan, but doesn't see why the man left his family in the first place, establishing yet another paradigm in the novel for a spiritual quest. Pictures of Washington and Lafayette and a copy of the Constitution place the house in its chronological period and identify the patriotic art and decor of a period American home, a subtle linkage of the family to the nation.

Emmeline Grangerford's artistic renderings of grieving women stand out in chapter 27. If Tom's use of the authorities as instructors for pirate action tended to discredit them, Emmeline's gruesome sentimentalizing undermines literary emotions as a basis for real feeling. Her dying ladies, each captioned with "Alas," are dark, and one with unfinished arms is "too spidery" for Huck, spiders already being signs of bad luck. Her verse, composed in a race with the undertaker, is travesty. This chapter finishes Twain's rejection of the shore world as a basis for real feeling as well as acting; the purpose lies underneath the surface color of the cultural burlesque of sentimental stereotypes. Huck reports that he spends time in Emmeline's room when her art "aggravates" him, and he even tries to write a memorial verse for her. This seemingly silly business reasserts Huck's allegiance with the suffering, the endangered, and the dead—despite his famous denial that he took no stock in dead people. The chapter reaffirms Huck's limitations as a naif, but not by degrading him to the level of a foulmouthed gutter urchin, whom we might reject. Twain uses the softer means of burlesque, so that we accept and even ignore the implied limitations of Huck's intellect.

Chapter 28 carries the action through the death of the Grangerfords and Huck's escape again to the raft—a fast-paced set of events that manages to define the violence of the feud, introduce ironic commentary on church, offer a Romeo-and-Juliet escape, and show Huck touched deeply but briefly by the death of Buck.

Dressed totally in white, with flashing black eyes, and standing straight as a liberty-pole, Colonel Grangerford is identified as a model of the first quality anywhere. The family is depicted similarly. Planter aristocracy, all the family are proud and each person "had their own nigger" to wait on them. They are "aristocracy," "high-toned," "well born", "rich and grand," "a handsome lot of quality"; Huck offers us a barrage of phrases to set their social place at the top of his world, with balls and picnics as their festivals. Even at family junkets, "the men brought their guns with them." The raftsmen's roughness appeared in ready brawling, but the violence of "the quality" appears in their proud bearing. The level of violence here is greater than on the flatboat; Huck came close to being painted blue on the flatboat, but not to being murdered as a Shepherdson. They are "another clan of aristocracy" and a "tribe," words that suggest their closeness to savages. Buck nearly kills Harney Shepherdson from ambush merely in a casual encounter. Harney "covers" Buck twice with his gun but does not shoot him, allowing us a measure of approval for Harney which will be paid off later. Twain the melodramatist uses foreshadowing to increase the pace of his action.

"Feud" as a concept is highlighted by a dialogue less blackface minstrel than portentous. Its violence, explained by Buck to Huck, appears as crazyness through the medium of Huck's supposedly naive questions. As with the battles on the flatboat, there is no significant reason for the feud. Once again, recalling the events of the first seven chapters, the problem is rooted in the failure of law to obtain justice, for the feud began when one side lost a court case and killed the man on the other side. Huck and Buck's discussion of the feud is another in the string of paradoxical minstrel-show dialogues that dot the first half of the book. Twain's development of these logical arguments begins to yield the full irony of what critic Walter Blair called the wise-fool way of arguing. A feud continues until everyone is killed off, and takes a long time. Worse, Buck, as he narrates, does not see what the reader easily sees. Outright murder becomes heroism when perpetrated by old baldy Shepherdson; an acceptable death results from bullet-holes in the front of an unarmed boy rather than in his back. Huck does not comment. A thoughtful reader might well understand how the Concord Library Board would object to the approval expressed by Buck.

As a mechanism to trigger the feud into violence, Twain develops a Romeo-and-Juliet episode, with Huck acting as go-between. Pretty Miss Sophia asks Huck to get her Testament—the first of the young girls Twain will use to establish the motif that will climax with Huck's aid to the Wilks girls. An element of manipulative seduction shows Miss Sophia asking Huck "if I liked her," and later giving him a squeeze. Huck's shrewdness is closely linked to his Pike vernacular: he slides out "quiet," reasons it "ain't natural for a girl to be in such a sweat" for a prayer book, and ransacks the prayer book to discover a hidden note. Huck is in disguise; Sophia uses and lies to Huck; Huck lies in return; concurrently, Huck's "nigger" lures him to Jim's hiding place in the swamp covertly by talking about snakes (later discussed by Huck and Jim as a shrewd manuever), and Huck, as deadpan as any modern tough-guy detective, follows noncommittally. These events are a truly remarkable compounding of withheld information; in this society, danger lies in openness. The veneer of lying, covering other evasions, suggests that Huck and Jim are not unique. Huck is enveloped in the behavior of paranoia, but the readers have seen real violence, and see more when Sophia runs off with Harney. Murder and chaos are the results. This is truly an awful world, stifled and repressed in ways that expand on the suppression of Huck's home village.

Hogs show up here, again, not in relation to Pap's hand, but in symphonic expansion representing men at church. In Twain's humorous passages, a comic view of social hypocrisy evolves from a universal sense of duplicity. Huck's description of the church—one of his funniest brief speeches—recasts experience in the terms of frontier social irony: "There warn't anybody at the church, except maybe a hog or two, for there warn't any lock on the door, and hogs like a puncheon floor in summertime because it's cool. If you notice, most folks don't go to church only when they've got to; but a hog is different." Comfort is, for Huck, the logical denominator of action; his relation to Jim has been built up through their easy enjoyment of food and dry beds together. Although Pap's hand was once the hand of a hog, he said, and hogs are not yet a positive image, they represent the opposite immediacy from social experience, and so will be referred to later in the novel.

Jim's success in the swamp raises further issues about social relationships of race and class. The raft was retrieved by Grangerford slaves, but Jim has commandeered it by warning them that they must not grab a young white gentleman's property—they will get a hiding for it. The suggestion of violence is casually tucked into Jim's conversation, with Twain's sense of realism at work again. Jim also used bribes of ten cents to make them "rich." Jack, the slave who took Huck to the swamp to see cottonmouths, is discussed for his cleverness at not allowing himself actually to become directly involved. Jack's small level of management corresponds to the higher levels of duplicity in Miss Sophia and Huck. As fantastic as Melville's man-of-war world in *White Jacket,* or Milton's hierarchies of Heaven in *Paradise Lost,* the levels of life on river and bank are Twain's social cosmos, his demonstration of a pervasive world order through corresponding levels of action. In concluding the incident, Jack is endorsed for his kindness and smartness *by Jim,* one of the novel's heroes, in a phrase that could typically be heard even in the South at least through the 1960s: "Dat Jack's a good nigger." In the casually discriminatory language of southern caste, the central figures share in the bigotry Twain depicts to mirror his general sense of human nature.

The conclusion of the feud comes quickly. Huck, scrambling up a tree, sees men cussing, yelling, and attempting to kill two young chaps who turn out to be Buck and a relative. Although Huck is characteristically glad that Miss Sophia and Harney escaped, Buck curses his failure to kill Harney, reestablishing his full complicity in the violence that ensues. The Shepherdsons surprise the boys, "singing out" "Kill them, kill them," forcing the boys to jump for the river. The murder of Buck is described as making Huck so sick he almost fell out of the tree, wishing he had "never come ashore to see such sights," which he still dreams about. Huck, in this key phrase, separates the shore and the raft—an important lead to the raft idyl developed in the following chapter; he also identifies himself as speaking in retrospect, identifying himself as a matured narrator expressing a continuing horror. Huck "cried a little" when covering the face of Buck, who was "mighty good to me," bringing his experience of death fully into his emotions. Huck escapes through a darkened shore and plantation to the raft, our anxiety heightened by Jim's moving the raft and hiding it for security, but scaring Huck, abandoned briefly in the melodramatic events of the blackening night.

The concluding paragraphs of the Grangerford chapters and the initial paragraphs of chapter 19, before the Duke and Dauphin successfully invade the raft, are a high point in Twain's depiction of a world. The raft is ennobled by its presence on the Mississippi River set apart from the shore towns. The comic sequences in which Huck and Jim formed their mode of life contribute an ethical dimension to a natural idyl on the river. The invasion of the raft forces Huck and Jim to further articulate the social philosophy of the raft, and this social philosophy will be restated in the last fifth of the novel. The center of the novel lies in chapter 19, especially if it is taken together with some elaborations of Jim's humanity as portrayed in chapter 23 about his daughter, and a few lines elsewhere.

As Huck escapes from the chaos of the feud and anxiously seeks the raft, its significance is sharpened in comparison with the shore. The unspeakableness of events is suggested when "a voice"—only a few tension-filled moments later identified as Jim's voice—responds to

Huck's desperate call. Huck tells Jim of "something up there" that will make people think he has been murdered—as Jim and Jack had feared. The loyalty of the raft, however, has been stronger for Jim than security, and as he hugs Huck in sign of physical welcome—for Twain, the localized physical response is the final determinant, as for church pigs—he explains that he was not leaving until he was "certain" Huck was killed. Thus, Jim responds for Huck as Huck had responded for Jim earlier when the slave-hunters had accosted him on the river.

Jim has again aided in securing Huck's welfare, and the moment offers the crucial ideas concerning freedom and safety. They shove off for the "big water," and old comfort but a newly matured sentiment. The alternative world is heightened by contrast with the minutely described milieu of the Grangerfords. Huck's feelings recall the original feeling of constraint in St. Petersburg versus freedom on Jackson's Island. They are "free and safe once more." Their "good time" is the opposite of the fear of discovery on the shore, and the only real antidote to Huck's loneliness. Twain moves the action quickly away from the Grangerford events to the real antidote. Huck and Jim conclude by codifying the philosophical underpinnings of the raft: "Other places do seem so cramped up and smothery, but a raft don't. You feel mighty free and easy and comfortable on a raft." Together, the white boy and black man, naked and secure, dangle their feet easily in the water of the quiet river. Still couched in the localist dialect with its awkward negatives, the statements reassert the ultimate American democratic values: free and easy.

Also, Huck says, for the first time, something that represents the brightest spot in the symphony now rising in power toward its climax, something, just at the end of his escape from the Grangerford experience, which he could not have said about the widow's and Miss Watson's, nor about Pap's cabin with its slovenly ease: "We said there warn't no home like a raft after all." And so, for the first time, Huck has a "home."

The raft idyl of chapter 19 is both the middle-class ideal and the workingman's dream. These heroes are common men with a workingman's yearning for time off; it happens that the time off is time off from the tension of social constraint and murderous contention, but it resonates for an American middle-class readership. These are days that swim or slide by "quiet and smooth and lovely." Sublime descriptions worthy of the great Romantic poets are blended with vernacular dialect: "the whole world was asleep, only sometimes the bull-frogs a-cluttering, maybe." In fact, Huck's description is worthy of an impressionist painting in its sense of blurred and richly colored detail.

Twain the post–Civil War realist is also at work. Details carry intense social criticism. First, social observation by Huck is only apparently pictorial: "a wood-yard, probably, and piled by them cheats so you can throw a dog through it anywheres." Second, low detail corresponds to the more conventional high beauty; echoing the ugly fish metaphor describing Pap's white skin, Huck notes, "they've left dead fish lying around, gars, and such, and they do get pretty rank." Add the second-person "you" of Huck's supposedly untrained narrative voice and a few localisms, and it is little wonder that Hemingway picked out the first four-fifths of *Huck Finn* as the root of modern American literature. The great mastery of language in the novel lies in Twain's transposing the language of the sublime into the language of the Pike. They "kind of lazy along," "lazy off to sleep," "lazying around, listening to the stillness." You'd see a "galoot" chopping wood, axe flashing, but only hear the "k'chunk" later. The language evolves a picture as sublime as any painted by the luminist painters, but without escaping from the realistic suggestions of workingmen in a civilized frontier setting. Thus, Huck responds with character-defining pragmatism to superstitous Jim about foggy spirits "carrying on that way in the air": "No, spirits wouldn't say, 'dern the dern fog.' " Testament to Twain's descriptive power in the vernacular is our sense as readers that the last line is comic—an anticlimax, showing the vulgar life of common men beneath the higher sensitivity now manifested by Huck and Jim.

Traveling nights, swimming naked (as mosquitos allow, notes Twain the realist, reassuring us that sentimental romantic nature is not involved in this realist natural beauty), Huck and Jim identify themselves with the starry sky above. In their most elevated natural experience, Huck, again free, from the confining clothes of the Grangerfords this time, describes the "whole river to ourselves" and the sparks of far-off lights, repeating "It's lovely to live on a raft." The star-speckled sky to Jim is "made" but to Huck "only just happened," yet another theological debate, but no longer the minstrel travesty of the one on Solomon. Huck allows Jim's suggestion that the moon could have laid the stars because he'd seen a frog "lay most as many." In the highest level of natural metaphor, Huck comes to describe his and Jim's condition: "We used to watch the stars that fell, too, and see them streak down. Jim allowed they'd got spoiled and was hove out of the nest." Thus united with nature, watching a steamboat at midnight throwing sparks out over the darkened river in celebration of the Mississippi, Huck and Jim achieve their fullest moment of secure isolation from the distant lights of life on the shore.

These moments represent the high point of Huck and Jim's independence on the raft. Out of the contentious materials of the widow Douglas's and Pap's teaching they have fabricated a pragmatic philosophy. They have protected each other and shared the lazy comforts of river freedom, centering on wholesome food, the vulnerable childhood nakedness of the ole swimmin' hole, stillness, and natural beauty. They have escaped crises and committed themselves to their goals of safety and freedom, even though, because of passing Cairo, Illinois, the simplest means of escape has eluded them. Their bond together has become stronger than the immediate plans they made in defining their trip.

Never again, after these great passages, will Huck and Jim's raft world be so idyllic. Several paragraphs after this, the entry of the Duke and Dauphin will give Huck cause to add further qualities to our sense of the raft and of Jim's humanity. First, Huck identifies a raft ethic in accommodating the two cheats. Second, another scene of Huck and Jim standing watch offers more insight into their relationship and leads to Jim's revelation of his treatment of his daughter—his most touchingly human moment. The raft ethic is finally completed after the tramps declare themslves royalty and seize control of the raft. Dominating the raft, they agree to cooperate. Huck summarizes: "It would have been a miserable business to have any unfriendliness on the raft, for what you want, above all things, on a raft, is for everybody to be satisfied, and feel right and kind towards the others." Many sophisticated concepts are implied in this simple speech: "above all things" establishes a higher law, "satisfied" suggests Jim and Huck's physical life separated from social dogma but allied to comfort, the denominator of "right" and "kind" as feelings for others—a remarkably graceful way of adapting the rigid philosophy of the widow and Miss Watson as previously burlesqued by Huck in the woods and after the *Walter Scott* episode. The raft ethic never appears better than when under domination by absolutist monarchy, however fraudulent.

A "watch" is stood by Huck and Jim in chapter 23, giving us further experience of Jim's easygoing kindness and providing an opportunity for the full statement of the raft ethic. Jim, in contrast to the selfishness of the Duke and Dauphin occupying the wigwam, takes Huck's watch. When a chance wave washes Huck overboard in the warm rain, Jim laughs—"he was the easiest nigger to laugh that ever was, anyway"—to Huck's annoyance. The line is another in which "nigger" is especially grating as evidence of a lowness in the hero-narrator in response to provocation. Yet the joke is a natural one, not contrived, and Jim's feelings are shown here in a way that will be deeply contrasted at the end of chapter 23. At that time, Jim again stands watch for Huck after they have discussed the hard lot of kings, samples of which have seized their raft. Huck awakes to hear Jim, head between his knees, moaning in sorrow for his wife and children. Huck comments, with ingenuousness intended by Twain to be representative of social premises but now almost too naive, "I do believe he cared just as much for his people as white folks does for theirn. It don't seem natural, but I reckon it's so." Obviously a notion held by society, this easy racist assumption fits comfortably with the idea that slaves should be grateful to their owners and not run away. "Natural" here, however, is the perversity of a Sut Lovingood, the southwestern clay-eater who is a natural darned fool.

Jim's only detailed personal story places him for us, and further comment by Huck is unnecessary, particularly as it was presented beforehand. He slaps his deaf daughter not knowing that she has lost her hearing from scarlet fever. Jim concludes, "O, Huck, I bust out a-cryin', en grab her up in my arms. . . . de Lord God Amighty fogive po' ole Jim, kaze he never gwyne to fogive hisseff." Hurting the innocent child, already "suffering," is an ultimate shame to Jim, corresponding to Huck's sympathy for rapscallions, but far more logical. Jim's unthoughtful harshness parallels the practical jokes Huck had earlier played on him, and closes the circle of action in which both Huck and Jim have experienced the consequences of socially accepted but thoughtless actions. Jim appeals to the Lord for forgiveness, suggesting the depth of his spiritual pain, a sincerity of feeling to be echoed by Huck with Mary Jane Wilks and in his final moments on the raft.

The conclusion of the portrayal of a raft-ethic identifies rightness and kindness as the denominators for relationships. These seemingly soft denominators are rather close to what Victorian Americans revered as true manliness, incidentally: King Arthur only becomes supremely great to Yankee Hank Morgan when he enters a smallpox hut and carries out a dying child in his arms. Kindness will figure centrally in Huck's decision for the Wilks girls even before he must make his decision for Jim. To Twain, as he demonstrated in virtually all his major novels, it is the appropriate antidote to authoritarian power and narrow literalism in social and religious doctrine. This individualized ethic is, of course, the ethic of a democracy more than any other form of political construction, and so on a deeper level his political and his humanitarian beliefs coincide. The machinery is now in place for the great decisions to come to Huck when his sound heart will overcome his deformed social conscience.

− 7 −

The Duke and Dauphin:
Authoritarian Fraud

Twain's later pessimism is so obvious that its consistency with points made throughout his canon is easily overlooked. At no time does Twain describe a happy state as a permanent one, and he views domestic happiness with irony. Twain's humor exploits the dichotomy between social/political ideals and selfishness. His similarity to predecessors like Artemus Ward can be traced to Ward's patriotic old showman, both a burlesque and projection of the ironic insight into humanity implied in the real figure of P. T. Barnum. In politics, the vision expresses itself first in burlesques of corruption, for which Twain became famous throughout the West in the 1860s, and later in pictures of greedy bluff, pretense, and outright thievery. *The Gilded Age* showed this in the U. S. Congress; *The Prince and the Pauper* showed it in the evil and mean Hugh Hendon; *A Connecticut Yankee* showed it in Morgan le Fay, the knights of the Round Table, and the Roman Catholic Church. In *Adventures of Huckleberry Finn*, we see the seizure of power through the fraud of inherited titles in the sham Duke and Dauphin who now come to dominate the raft. In its denial of Huck and Jim's aspirations even as they rise in humanity, the novel now takes on the potential for tragedy.

As Huck and Jim's raft idyl reaches its high point, a couple of men escaping pursuit beg Huck to save them, "said they hadn't been doing nothing, and was being chased for it." The laconic skepticism tells us that Huck knew from their first speech that the two men were fakes, but he contrives a successful escape by water for them anyway. The two men will take control of the raft just as *The Gilded Age* described southerners retaking control of the Federal government after the Civil War. False aristocracy is at home anywhere and moves directly to claim power. A series of events deriving from their presence will show that the bottom and the top of the social scale are one, for just like Pap in their drunkenness they also represent outcast kings and Shakespeare. Twain's Whittier Birthday Dinner speech in 1877 had attempted a similar uniting of all levels of society, but had failed in an inappropriate setting. Here, laid out along the path of Mississippi River villages representing the commonality of the American heartland, the travesty at last finds its proper setting. Events will now race, counterpointed by the raft refuge, from the Boggs-Sherburn episode through the camp meeting and the Royal Nonesuch at Bricksville, and on to the climactic Wilks episode and the finish of Huck and Jim's raft at Pikesville, a few miles above the Phelps Farm. The first events stand as one group, with the Wilks family episode, itself the longest and most revealing episode in Huck's travels, standing as a separate event.

On the Mississippi, where Huck and Jim have already discussed kings both biblical and historical, the privileges of absolute power—monarchical power—are endowed with controlling force due to the credulousness of the victims. Coupled now with the absolutism of religion and social custom, the absolutism of authoritarian political power will be demonstrated through the caricature Duke and Dauphin. Concurrently, Twain will offer us his greatest indictment of the levelling commonness of the small town—the village mentality limited, selfish, and cruel—through his portraits of the lynch mob, the camp meeting, and the circus and theater entertainments. Democracy at this level will not even be permitted to offer an alternative: only the raft as we the readers now remember it will constitute that alternative.

The Duke and the Dauphin also represent one of Twain's finest thematic elaborations. At the very moment that the raft is reaching its highest ethical development, the burlesque minstrel routines concerning monarchs are translated syllogistically into real travesties of royalty. As Huck and Jim define what they are, their physical world is usurped from them. The symphonic expansion of this proceeding continues in the last fifth of the novel, following Huck's greatest speech of all, with Tom Sawyer. There, on the brink of real unity of purpose, Huck and Jim are lowered into travesty through Tom's control. It is the moment when the Duke and Dauphin seize the raft that establishes the pattern for this later, larger defeat. Twain's plot is pessimistic here, not optimistic, about the perfectability of society, and it is perhaps for this reason that the darker aspects of this progression are overlooked in the seemingly happy boy's book, and construed by analytic critics as a failure in form.

The Duke and Dauphin on entrance are unprepossessing even to Huck. Both are dressed "ornery," as Huck details their country clothes. Both are clearly small-time scoundrels preying on people more ignorant then themselves—one removing tartar from teeth but taking the enamel with it, the other doing good "business" as a temperance revivalist, but caught drinking and now on the run to escape being tarred and feathered. Preying on women and children is a particularly characteristic action for the pair, later expanded in the camp meeting and Wilks episodes. The first elaborates his "line" as patent-medicines, theater-acting, mesmerism, phrenology, singing school and geography, and "anything that comes handy, so it ain't work." The second, older man specializes in laying on of hands to cure cancer and paralysis, fortune-telling, and preaching at camp meetings and missionarying around, as he puts it: "Layin' on o' hands is my best holt." As with the slave-hunters, disease for others is a matter of indifference in comparison to money, but here it is more predatory. The men prey on pain and illness; their shiftiness and role-playing is not comparable to that of Huck and Jim. It takes advantage of and damages others for profit; it is more evil than the chameleon evasiveness of Huck and Jim. It is the most sinister adult form of the practices of . . . . Tom Sawyer.

Immediately, as the two "beats" settle themselves on Huck and Jim's raft, the younger man takes to "alassin' " about his fate and both men announce themselves as banished royalty, establishing in the central action Twain's bête noir, monarchical authority. The mentality of absolutism can easily be treated in burlesque, since even in noncaricature, as in *The Prince and the Pauper*, much of the absurdity of royalty is shown either in egregious melodrama or in ironically described events and slapstick. To Twain open fraudulence claiming monarchal authority for personal gain is merely comic shorthand for historical fact.

Manipulating the language of cheap romances, against a counterpoint of skepticism from the old man, the young man reveals that he has been brought down from his rightful place as the Duke of Bridgewater. The Duke's revelation is false, but it makes Huck and Jim momentarily credulous, and they agree to solace him by calling him "Your Grace." The older man, angry, then takes hold of the false pretension to announce himself as the rightful heir to the throne of France, "in blue jeans and misery." The Dauphin counsels the now sulky Duke to accept his lower status, for he can still usurp the raft's ease—"plenty grub and an easy life." Royalty arrogates to itself the goods and earned wealth of the lower class; the Duke and king's acts are a microcosm of Twain's view of authoritarian power in government. Tom Sawyer will do likewise, rising to ever crazier heights of pretension in the "evasion."

Huck, as noted earlier, accommodates this reconciliation within the raft ethic. The Dauphin successfully cajoles the Duke, "It ain't my fault I warn't born a duke. . . . Make the best o' things the way you find 'em, says I." Huck and Jim, in turn, declare their gladness to see the handshaking reconciliation, and they expose their raft ethic now in subordination to a falsely imposed political power: "We felt mighty good over it, because it would a been a miserable business to have any unfriendliness on the raft, for what you want, above all things, on a raft, is for everybody to be satisfied, and feel right and kind towards the others." With this statement, Huck identifies the higher law of humanity (above all things) that has made his relationship with Jim a uniquely personal adventure. Here it becomes the property of the locus "raft." Now, we as readers truly understand that we have an independent and specially defined world, even as it succumbs to the vulnerability of all places in the world to control by the politically corrupt.

Huck also reveals his own insight, casting a strange and doubtful light over his failure to protect the raft in the first place. He comments that he knew that the liars were "low-down humbugs and frauds." However, he keeps silent so as not to cause trouble, to "keep peace in the family"—a slanting reference to the P. T. Barnum Museum's "Happy Family" where the lamb and lion occupied the same cage. Olive Logan, a showwoman and platform lecturer influenced by Artemus Ward, had long before revealed, in *The Mimic World* (1871), that Barnum's effect was achieved by having the lion secretly drugged with morphine. Everything about this expression of ethics is thus problematical, and it becomes more so. Huck says, "If I never learnt nothing else out of pap, I learnt that the best way to get along with his kind of people is to let them have their own way." We recall that Huck could well have been murdered by his drunken Pap. Huck is thus in the most passive position possible for a free man; only his status as a boy allows for this philosophical passivity to be fictionally convincing. So Huck does not tell Jim and is willing to call the fake nobility by their titles. Such a philosophy almost assures us of the necessity for Huck's final decision at the end of the book to flee to "the Territories." Linked to Pap, the rapscallions are linked to, and imply a taint of, St. Petersburg.

The identification of the raft world is complete. The portion of the novel occupied by the Duke and the Dauphin—eleven of forty-three chapters—will now restate and expand the major themes of the novel. The indictment of religion is broadened negatively through the camp meeting sequence and positively through Mary Jane Wilks's endorsement of Huck. The vulgar venality of the American small town is elaborated through Bricksville and the Royal Nonesuch sequence. Separate from the minor swindles of the Duke and Dauphin, but within this framework, comes the indictment of lynch law, social order and religion, and human psychology presented in the Boggs-Sherburn and the circus episodes. The episode around the Wilks girls in which Huck foils the Duke and the Dauphin compensates the reader for the loss of the raft and Jim's freedom to Tom, but foreshadows the feeling that determines Huck's ultimate flight from civilization.

Seemingly minor actions foreshadow major events terminating this section of the novel. The first is the questioning of Huck about Jim as a "runaway nigger." Huck puts this off by asking would a runaway nigger run South? But the sense of Jim as vulnerable to the Duke is established, even though the Duke is even more threatened by disclosure than is Jim, fearing to pass a nearby town in daylight because it "mightn't be healthy."

A second motif is established as we see the Duke and Dauphin as usurpers of the rightful goods of others. They renovate Huck and Jim's wigwam, arguing over who gets which bed and finally deciding the question based on social rank, although the close detail of Huck's description of the shuck bed makes clear the lowering of the individuals who so argue. In comparison, Huck and Jim share another fleeting moment of comradeship. Jim stands Huck's watch, but Huck is forced to sleep on deck because the Duke and Dauphin have taken over the whole wigwam. When Huck is washed overboard by a wave, Jim almost kills himself laughing, "He was the easiest nigger to laugh that ever was anyway." Both a racist remark and a human one, it denotes the tenor of Jim's life, consistent with the wonderful heroine of Twain's "A True Story," where laughter and seeming joy are a triumph over deeper past sorrows.

Last, the king and Duke must "lay out a campaign." A further cultural travesty finds the king playing Juliet in *Romeo and Juliet*. The Duke's arrogance is plain when he claims the "country jakes" will not even notice the Dauphin's whiskers and bald head as heroine. They begin practicing Shakespeare and land at a little town where the Duke heads for a printing office and the Dauphin falls into a "sick nigger" who informs him of a camp meeting. Thus ends the segue from the world of the raft to the world of the shore, now to be brought to crescendo and climax in a series of degraded social portraits.

The camp meeting is the first of several shows—Shakespeare, the circus, and the Royal Nonesuch will follow—appealing to popular instincts, and the Dauphin's response is to regard it as a show in which he can play the dominant role. In this, the character follows closely Captain Simon Suggs, a figure who dominated a similar show, as depicted in *Some Adventures of Captain Simon Suggs, Late of the Tallapoosa Volunteers* (1845), written by southwestern humorist Johnson Jones Hooper prior to the Civil War. Simon, a hoary-headed sinner, observes skeptically that since "nater is nater," the preachers save the pretty women first. He outdoes their performance of conversion, collects a large donation to found a church, and escapes through a swamp, pretending to pray and taking the money with him. He concludes with the sentiment "live and let live," since the preachers had a show almost as good as Suggs's own.

Twain uses similar elements in his camp-meeting sequence. The worshipers are gradually worked into a frenzy by their singing. When the Bible is "spread" open by the yelling preacher, the scene borrows some of the aspects of the "spread-eagle" prancing of the Duke and Dauphin practicing their grotesque version of Shakespeare. In Hooper's version, men and women lay in "promiscuous" heaps. Here they are worked into a passion through a preacher's ranting; they are "crazy and wild," but the sense of scene is similar. The Duke and Dauphin have just degraded Shakespeare's rhetoric, and the religious rhetoric here seems similarly degraded. Like Simon Suggs, the Dauphin claims a conversion and somebody "sings" out to take up a collection (the previous "sing out" was "Kill Them! Kill Them!" directed at Buck Grangerford, so the word itself carries an unpleasant overtone now).

The prettiest girls kiss the Dauphin, as many as five or six times, but he declines offers to stay the week, so that he can return to the pirates and convert them. He declares to Huck later that heathens "don't amount to shucks" compared to pirates in order to "work" a camp-meeting. To the Dauphin religion is a vehicle for profit, and since he steals a jug of whiskey on his way out of the camp meeting, he is hardly the only hypocritical sinner so abusing this medium.

Having revealed the socially elevated side of religion through the widow Douglas and Miss Watson, Twain has now shown the low side. If Huck's skepticism was justified by seeing Tom show the marks of a Sunday school and by the failure of the doctrine of gifts to make pragmatic sense, he now sees the lowest social reality. Religion is another grade of fraud practiced on the vulgar by the cynical; it has vaguely sensual elements directed at women. Sophia's psalm book carried the note that triggered the murders of her family; old Boggs will have a heavy Bible placed on his chest as he dies; the mass of common men indulge in self-degrading excesses and are defrauded of their money. Visually, Twain's camp-meeting scene is the most fully realized attack on folk religion, but it will be expanded naturally into a further burlesque when the Dauphin becomes the minister-brother of Peter Wilks. Already, here, the work is well under way which defines the bad side of religion. The way is also now clear for Huck and Mary Jane Wilks to respond to the widow's alternative to the punishing Providence— Twain's unstructured view of religious sublimity as finally developed in gentle individual recognitions.

While Huck and the King have been attending the camp meeting, the Duke has set up a handbill describing Jim as a runaway "nigger" with a $200 reward. The fake reward is now $100 less than the real reward at the start of the novel. Jim will be tied "hand and foot" as necessary, since handcuffs would be like jewelry and, appropriate to the culture of literary drama paying obeisance to Shakespeare, "we must preserve the unities." At the end of chapter 20, Jim even comes to protest against more kings, since the present crop is drunk, and Huck tells us that the one had said he had "forgot" his native language. The flagrancy of the frauds will next be translated to literature and culture, and finally to humanity.

The travesty of Shakespeare establishes the progression from earlier travesties toward Tom's greatest efforts at the end of the novel. So crass is it that the King must be counselled not to "bray like a jackass." Huck says it "knocked the spots" off any acting he had seen, defining the level of culture in his world, and aligning himself with it. Their bill as posted in Bricksville is the appropriate travesty of culture to introduce us to Twain's most completely realized portrait of the small town. Here presented as an Arkansas artifact, it is actually Twain's portrait of mass man in the common setting generally.

Twain, having dramatized the worst aspects of religious authority, turns his attention to social authority in two forms: the aristocratic code of honor as practiced by Colonel Sherburn and the degraded code of unregulated lynch law as seen in the Bricksville loafers. First, however, he describes the town, dilapidated physically and morally—vulgarity at its least redeemable. In a setting of low cruelty, Huck's brand of ignorance differs from the townspeople's, although Twain will take care to connect him to them after Boggs is shot and the circus occurs. "Shackly," weedy, ashes and junk surround unpainted houses: the town is an emblem of neglect, where fences—"whitewashed . . . in Clumbus's time"—are the opposite of Tom Sawyer's home fence. The paragraphs that follow are perhaps Twain's deepest descent into vulgar realism in his novels, and reading them suggests why a book which contains them might be considered a poor instructor for youthful readers. Loafers chaw, gap, yawn, and stretch—they are a "mighty ornery lot" to Huck's now practiced eye. Their cussing denominates their low status, as does their borrowing of tobacco, their lying and arguing. Using nature's products by borrowing them from each other, there is no indication that they actually do any work to grow them. If Pap Finn was a single muddy individual, the town's streets expand the idea by being "nothing else *but* mud" occupied by a hog feeding her piglets, "as happy as if she was on salary." A running diction of economics suggests weak money alliances—back "intrust" will be paid for a chaw, complementing the salary reference. Store tobacco is defined against "nigger-head"—both a local color opportunity and a chance to emphasize the lowness of country economics and show the unappetizing loafers in mental action.

Cruelty defines this world, emanating from its local country characters. Pap's cruelty was directed in malice at Huck; the loafers' is generalized. They delight in seeing dogs attack the sow feeding piglets (an obvious image of nurturing) and encourage the attack—as opposed to Huck who merely observed pigs' sincerity in church. They torture stray dogs to death. Huck and Jim are strays, and the highest poetic moment in the novel implied their likeness to shooting stars; this absolutely degraded low cruelty is the symbolic alternative, and this correspondence gives the Bricksville passages their significant place in the emotional world of the novel. When Colonel Sherburn accuses the mob of being able only to tar and feather poor and friendless fallen women, he will not only expand our sense of this cruelty to the human level, he will lay down crucial foreshadowing of a later moment when Huck will define human action in terms of the better ethic of the raft. In the final capture and tarring and feathering of the Duke and the Dauphin, later, such village cruelty will be made a component of the dramatic action to which Huck must respond. Here, a paragraph even appears that suggests that the river is in opposition to the town—physically as much as the raft and town are opposed emotionally—as the river forces "such a town" to be always "moving back, and back, and back."

Three fights and whiskey-drinking lead directly, by means of a dash as punctuation, to an unnamed voice who shouts out that Boggs has come in from the country for his "little old monthly drunk." The following sentence, "All the loafers looked glad," identifies Boggs's appearance as an escalation of cruelty, and Huck comments that they seemed used to having fun out of Boggs. In fact, the episode does more than that, for it further defines social "quality" as murderous in comparison to the rough naivete of a country drunkard and his innocent daughter. The scene is particularly effective because the violence of the loafers is transferred to Colonel Sherburn and then reenacted by the townspeople. The notes of the symphony appear in varying configurations, and the development of meaning continues.

Old Boggs is clearly unthreatening, despite his manner. Before he even enters, a loafer wishes Boggs would threaten him and make him feel safe for a thousand years, since Boggs never fulfills his threats. His boasts are comic, following in the manner of the battling flatboatmen—less real violence and more clearly frontier local color—as he yells that the price of coffins is going to rise. "Everyone" yells at Boggs and laughs and sasses him, and he offers a second colorful phrase about Colonel Sherburn: "meat first, and spoon vittles to top off on." Thus, the suggestion is strong that Col. Sherburn is not actually threatened. A third suggestion of Boggs's harmlessness is offered when Huck is reassured, "He don't mean nothing; he's always carryin' on like that, when he's drunk. He's the best-naturedest old fool in Arkansaw—never hurt nobody, drunk nor sober." To readers then, Boggs is unlikely to require punishment either by a character or through symbolic action like what happens to Pap after the "Call this a govment" speech. He is differentiated from those who would perpetrate violence by his nature and the diminutives applied to him—"old fool," "little" drunk, and the like.

Nevertheless, the force set against Boggs is aligned with the same social standing that accounted for the feud, and Colonel Sherburn will shoot down Boggs in cold blood. Owning the "biggest" store in town, Sherburn is a "proud-looking" man and the best-dressed man in town, qualities that relate him to Colonel Grangerford, and is likewise designated a member of the regional aristocracy by his title. Based on a murder in Hannibal, Missouri, during Twain's childhood, the Boggs incident is transmuted into a representation of the arrogance of caste and class. Miss Watson's aggression toward Huck is replayed and expanded as murderous physical aggression among adults.

As in the other scenes of the novel, the melodrama of the event is fully developed. Sherburn moves toward Boggs with calmness and slowness. His threat to Boggs to stop by one o'clock is couched in the threatening language of an unremitting vendetta. The "men" take his threat seriously and attempt, humanly enough, to quiet Boggs and remove him from real danger. Boggs, however, goes "a-raging" back and forth, escalating the opposition. His daughter is sent for and is described as being brought to the scene even as Sherburn murders her father standing unarmed and pleading for mercy in the street.

The event is as remarkable as it is horrible. Twain uses all his skill as a melodramatist to heighten the tension of the moment. Language such as "a-raging" to describe Boggs asserts escalating hatred between Boggs and Sherburn—false to the actual incident. Once again an unnamed voice (although obviously Sherburn's)—as Twain described Jim's first call to Huck after the Shepherdson killings—"sings out" one word: "Boggs!" Sherburn's gun barrel is described as pointed at the sky, then slowly—and steadily—lowered, with the same feeling of fatality that accreted around Grangerford's temper and the feud itself. Rather than describing the action, Huck says, "Bang!"—giving a sound-effect and describing the daughter rushing forward to exclaim over Boggs, "Oh, he's killed him." The action then shifts to the crowd who crane and push to see the dying man. Even Col. Sherburn's exit is contemptuous. Colonel Sherburn is coldly arrogant, but he is not criticized in any way that challenges his level of human insight. Nonetheless, he is clearly separated from the human insight gained by Huck in the space of seconds in the previous two pages. The dragging off of the daughter after Boggs's death completes the melodrama of injured innocence, for she is sixteen and "very sweet and gentle-looking, but awful pale and scared."

Once the melodrama of injured innocence is complete, Twain again indicts the villagers as creatures of vulgar curiosity. The crowd now participates in the murder as they push in to gape at the dying man. Huck is implicated by getting a "good" place before the drug-store window where Boggs is taken. A heavy Bible is placed on the dying man's chest, implicating religiosity along with curiosity. As well, since Twain's concept of the "village" mentality is that it distorts both religion and politics, the whole town comes "scrounging and pushing" to see the body, and latecomers complain that " 'taint right and 'taint fair, for you to stay thar all the time . . . other folks has their rights as well as you." Thus, democratic "rights" are introduced again into lo-calized violence in the same terms used on the *Walter Scott* previously by the leader of the thieves. The village setting shows democratic rights in their distorted use by the selfish, not in the ideal form that Twain ultimately admired. The tall man in a stovepipe hat who reen-acts the killing is "treated" as if at an election; the last reference to such a hat was during Pap's attack on the govment, in which he was also drinking. Echoes of the previous event are the means by which Twain implies a failing in the democracy without opening up either a didactic discussion or a more overt series of democratic images forced into the event. Again, Twain can be recognized as the consummate American realist writer, including in a narrative of events the subtle details of implied social criticism in what first appears merely as ob-servation of scene.

Colonel Sherburn defines the town even more directly than Colonel Grangerford represents aristocracy. In his speech to the cowardly townspeople's lynch mob, he even describes it to itself. Since his speech was originally placed in *Life On the Mississippi* as Twain's own anal-ysis of North and South, it is worthy of special note. Huck is again implicated by accompanying the mob that goes to confront the mur-derer and lynch him.

The lynch mob, trivialized even by the detail of stealing clothes-lines for nooses, rages toward Sherburn's house. Described as a mob and a wave, the group of people has power only by its mass. Swarm-ing, making girls cry in an echo of Boggs's daughter, attracting and repelling young bucks and wenches, the crowd is as monstrous as Sherburn. Sherburn's isolated, calm, and deliberate stance on his own porch roof is both dramatic and symbolic. His speech draws out the point as he stares down individuals and makes them look "sneaky." His reference point is to one of the great polarizing concepts of Victorian literature, the power of a single "man." Artemus Ward in one burlesque interview counselled Prince Albert Edward of England to "be as good a man as your mother has been." Lincoln wrote to his friends to tell them there was a "man" in the presidency, with the same comic force, but without the element of burlesque.[13] For Sherburn, being a man represents a complex of power and fearlessness which is the opposite of the lynch mob with its "half-a-man" named Buck Harkness and the opposite, also, of an army, which is described as "borrowing" its courage from its mass and its officers. Even in this Mississippi setting, Twain attacks militarism. This identification of a "man" with Sherburn, unfortunately, bars the term from positive use. Here it is notably cold-blooded; Twain will not redeem it until he has Hank Morgan create "man factories" in Arthurian England. The strongest counterpoint remaining to be developed for Huck will be Mary Jane Wilks.

The attempt to lynch Colonel Sherburn for his cold-blooded murder of the inoffensive Boggs is a centerpiece in Twain's indictment of all facets of the small-town mentality. Its religion and politics corrupt the ideal states of higher reverence and democratic expression, relegating them, as in Hadleyburg later, to the realm of the abstract. Sherburn's speech identifies itself as a national rather than regional commentary, for Twain had been turning the problem of law and justice over in his mind for some time. Only a few years earlier he had suppressed these sentiments from *Life On the Mississippi* because he felt that they would destroy his popularity in the South. In Sherburn's voice the reporter's sentiments are revised and presented in dramatic form, with the added advantage that the change in use forces him to drop a distinction he saw between the regions, thereby making Sherburn's speech a national and therefore universal indictment. In the cancelled passages from *Life On the Mississippi*[14] Twain muses on the "solid" political South, proposing that although it might appear savage, it was not really, and the horror of African slavery was gone. North and South are alike in the universal timidity of their people, but in the South a few hot-heads are more active than in the North where training, heredity, and fear of the law keep men under better command. The southern hot-head successfully defies the community, and although he is thinking of outlaws, his comment applies well to Sherburn. Southern juries are afraid to convict murderers, but lynch mobs go in masks. Twain even describes how a single Kentuckian held up a stageful of people, some armed, and concludes that the riders were like the "average" of the human race, "not plucky, but timid." In the North, timid fellows band together in the case of murderers to secure legal justice: "the average Southerners do not band themselves together in these high interests, but leave them to look out for themselves unsupported; the results being unpunished murder, against the popular approval, and the decay and destruction of independent thought and action in politics." Thus, Twain's analysis of regional human nature is in fact a politically oriented one.

The Sherburn episode takes on a social-political perspective in light of the *Life On the Mississippi* passage. The scene manifests Twain's concept of southern habits expanded, with the crowd reduced to savagery. The crowd is cowed by Sherburn, who even refers to the Kentucky incident: "In the south one man, all by himself, has stopped a stage full of men, in the day-time, and robbed the lot." Undoubtedly, Twain is carrying his premise into the texture of *Huck Finn*, but here as an accusation by a murderer representing the "quality"; the whole social order is indicted by this episode. The abrupt ending of the lynching sequence, with Huck going to the circus, is Twain's dramatic representation—with all its abruptness—of the short attention span and indifference of the public. The vain and idle law-abiding elements are willing to leave the interests of justice "to look out for themselves unsupported." The envelope of the lynching sequence suggests the earlier attack on human nature in the guise of a regional critique, and Sherburn's speech completes the statement.

Colonel Sherburn confronts the mob from his porch roof, above them, threateningly "ca'm and deliberate." He offers them a full analysis of lynch law, following a creepy stillness and a "sort of" laugh. He says they do not have the pluck to lynch a *man*, bringing forth the ideas of timidity and pluck as stated in the Kentucky incident, where Twain also used the word "pluck." He attacks juries that always acquit, "because they're afraid the man's friends will shoot them in the back," another comment leveled by Twain at the South previously. However, Sherburn raises the level of commentary by saying, "I was born and raised in the south, and I've lived in the north; so I know the average all around. The average man's a coward." Sherburn even draws the church in, when he says that the timid northerner goes home and prays for a humble spirit to bear being walked over. The original social analysis as roughed out in *Life On the Mississippi* is broadened to fit the themes of distorted religion and politics reversed to the service of bad causes. Sherburn's final declamation against the hundred masked cowards who come in the dark led by a half-man is punctuated with the definition of an "army" as a mob borrowing courage from its mass and its officers—a comment far afield from the interests of *Huck Finn,* but appropriate to a universal statement condemning the politics of American civilization. Sherburn's speech makes the culture of the river towns into an emblem of the average of the human race. Twain's pessimistic sentiments, of course, are cloaked by being placed not in Huck's mouth but in the mouth of a man of southern quality whom Huck observes, fears, and, of course, respects, by implication, since he corresponds to Colonel Grangerford. The novel seems to remain idealistic because Sherburn is distanced from Huck.

The transition to the circus is purposefully abrupt. Justice, ill-served by the lynch mob, is simply abandoned. Huck could have stayed if he had wanted, but in comic anticlimax, he says he didn't want to. The flatness of the transition is as degrading to our opinion of Huck as are the burlesque arguments with Jim. Huck is, in the town, no better than his world. In transition to the circus episode, he sneaks into the circus, even though he has the money to pay, since "you" might actually need the money later and there isn't any reason to "waste" money on "them." He thus continues the comic level of action, reenacting stories of rubes avoiding admission fees and cheating Barnum.[15] Huck retreats to the level of a stock comic figure so that Twain may then present him as credulous toward the circus trickery.

The circus impresses Huck with its beautiful glitter. The best defined business is the intrusion of a drunk into the riding ring. Almost beat up by the audience, he is allowed by the ringmaster to ride a horse. After seeming almost to get killed, he throws off his clothes to become the most gorgeous circus acrobat of all. To Huck alone, "it warn't funny . . . I was all a-tremble to see his danger," as the drunk tries to ride. Huck feels "sheepish" to have been taken in, but delights in how the "sick" ringmaster was also taken in, leaving the crowd "howling" with pleasure and astonishment. He allows that this "bully" circus can have all of his custom anytime. The scene reechoes the Boggs-Sherburn episode, but now as a calculated fraud. Hidden proficiency, impugned by the violent mass, bursts out as Tom Sawyer's devices will (and Huck's will not), to become entertainment. This event, unlike the Boggs-Sherburn event, is controlled; it offers a microcosm of Tom's freeing of Jim. With Huck it is a matter of real danger and ultimate acts of humanity; later, with Tom, a less imposing but more crowd-pleasing circus show becomes real life.

The Royal Nonesuch offers the final degradation of such shows, translating an old man (a mirror of both Boggs and the Dauphin) into a striped animal unworthy of respect. The Duke and Dauphin's fraudulent lowering of Shakespeare attracts only twelve "Arkansaw lunkheads," so the Duke determines to offer "something ruthur worse than low comedy." His ultimate lowering strategy is to announce on his poster, "Ladies and children not admitted," with the declaration: "There, if that line don't fetch them, I don't know Arkansaw!" The ultimate appeal to innocence is finally a degraded appeal to vulgarity. This one line alone helps account for the distaste that Opie Read's *The Arkansaw Traveler* and other local newspapers showed for the novel in 1885, but Arkansas here obviously represents a level of consciousness as much as a physical locale for Twain.

In the Royal Nonesuch, a borrowing by Twain of a western idea, "The Guyascutus," the Dauphin prances around the stage, starknaked, painted all over with rainbow stripes. Twain knew the story and even referred to himself in 1874 (letter to W. D. Howells, dated 4 December) as feeling happy that he did not have to prance around striped and stand on his head for the *Atlantic Monthly* audience then reading "Old Times on the Mississippi," precursor to the book *Life on the Mississippi*. Huck reports that people just killed themselves laughing at the king, but when the act is over, the crowd realizes it has been "sold" and is prevented from lynching the two frauds only by a twist in vanity that is allied to the timidity of the lynch mob. Specifically, the town's judge counsels the crowd to deceive everyone else into being fooled the same way so as not to be embarrassed. Thus, lawful authority feeds vanity. On the third night, the crowd plans to pelt the king with rotten vegetables and dead cats, but it is defeated by the Duke's cynicism, a low and vulgar reprise of the loftier arrogance of Colonel Sherburn; to the Duke they are merely "Greenhorns, flatheads" whose petty duplicity and revenge is predictable. The frauds take the gate receipts on the third night and sneak out of town, leaving a yokel to watch the door.

The chapter concludes with a discussion of royalty—"kings is kings, and you got to make allowances"—which puts monarchy at the level of "business is business" as an apology for mean practices, followed by Jim's account of his mistreatment of his daughter. The dialogue on kings expands on their murders, thereby increasing the sense of authoritarian murderousness beyond the single murders and lynchings committed by the commonality. The discussion, in the burlesque format of Huck and Jim's previous discussions, takes on a second level of meaning, for it is based on the bad-smelling, "mighty ornery" pair that Huck and Jim have inherited, rather than the worse lot represented by "Henry the Eight." In Huck's confused history, Henry also gains responsibility for the Boston Tea Party and the Declaration of Independence, extending the sense of kingship to America, just as the overall rapscallion nature of kings includes the Duke and the Dauphin. Huck's political comment represents Twain on monarchy: "I wish we could hear of a country that's out of kings." Huck concludes that there was no use to tell Jim the Duke and king's nobility is false since it, first, "wouldn't a done no good," and second, "you couldn't tell them from the real kind." An episode that begins as an examination of lynch law thus ends as an indictment of monarchy. Generalizing the thematic action of the novel, such developments render authority and authoritarian behavior irresponsible. Although such behavior would be checked by active democracy, human timidity—first in cowardly violence, second in embarrassment at exposure—offers no check, to the "quality," to royalty (circus or real), or to the rapscallions masquerading in barely credible royal disguise. Jim's unknowing cruelty in his own family presents a contrast by its sincere repentance. Violence exists at every level of life in the story—town, world, theater, circus entertainment, and family. At the individual level—that of Jim and Huck—it may be discovered and overcome by a kind heart. At higher levels of social action, we see no such cure.

— 8 —

The Wilks Episode: Huck and Mary Jane

The Wilks episode is initiated by events that begin to reduce Jim from a human level down to the level of a comic slave, a necessary foreshadowing of the end sequences of the novel. He becomes a painted grotesque and is removed from the action. The sequence concludes with the return of Jim to captivity on the Phelps Farm through the final low treachery of the king. In between, the royalty become religious frauds, impersonating lost heirs and taking in townspeople for whom all events are circuslike. They successfully prey on the very evidences of pride and innocence which characterize other families already presented. Only their greed in turn sets up the machinery that allows Huck to fulfill his ultimate moral destiny by deciding to free Jim for good. Religion receives further sharp licks from Twain in the Wilks episode, as the Duke and Dauphin pretend to represent it and Huck is validated by Mary Jane—our highest specimen of womanly humanity—even at the moment that he sees himself as a Judas betraying the social law of his region. She reinforces Huck as he defeats the villains. We thus come to the ultimate moment when Twain demonstrates the sound heart of a boy overcoming his deformed social conscience.

At the transition chapters 23 and 24 Jim appears at his highest and lowest points. Concluding the earlier chapter, Jim repents of his unknowing cruelty to his deaf daughter. Jim's humanity is thus fully revealed to Huck and the readers in an important vignette outside the plot of the story. The following chapter shows Jim reduced by the Duke and Dauphin to a blue-painted "sick arab"—a clown figure in the garb of King Lear—as Twain continues his travesty use of Shakespeare. Thus, Jim reaches his high and low points almost simultaneously, consistent with a novel that will reduce the overall relationship between Huck and Jim to Tom Sawyer's level just after Huck has made his ultimate decisions.

Huck is bound to the Duke and Dauphin by his own psychology of avoiding confrontations. He is dominated, of course, by their power over him—the power of authoritarian royalty, age and adulthood, parental force, superior meanness. Twain presents his hero as the victim of a full measure of underlying human forces controlling human nature. The fraudulence of the claim to monarchy enhances the awfulness of the control rather than undercuts it. I have not dwelt on Huck's own psychological history; suffice it to say that the adult men control Huck, repress his better senses, and finally abuse Huck and Jim emotionally. Jim only partly fulfills Huck's need for male kinship, and Tom Sawyer, the flamboyant, is worse in fulfilling this need. In the coming chapters we will also see Huck's need for female love in the figure of Mary Jane Wilks. At an underlying level, Twain's "repression of self" may very well account for Huck's pervasive passivity and his despair over personal worthlessness. (See Barchilon and Kovel as cited in the bibliography for one excellent reading along psychoanalytic lines.) This deeper reading parallels Twain's expression of political and social protest and his democratic philosophy at the intellectual level.

The most important components of the Wilks episode lie in four areas: first, the reindictment of the foolish "townspeople," the representative average men of the Mississippi River experience; second, the projection of the Duke and Dauphin, and like them, the undertaker—all travesties of conventional piety and respect; third, the greed of the Duke and Dauphin, which brings about their defeat; fourth, Huck's response to Mary Jane Wilks's kindness and his action to save her and her sisters from the Duke and Dauphin's rascality. Huck here lays the groundwork, through his decision to tell the truth, for his most important moment of moral reasoning, on the subject of Jim's freedom, which he must carry out between leaving the Wilks girls and arriving at the Phelps Farm. Throughout weaves the decreasingly wry humor of Huck, which begins in this sequence to become subordinate to the demonstration of events; after the end of the sequence, in chapter 31,

Huck's great moral decision will be made explicit, not implicit, and though the reader will need to see the irony of the human and moral reversals that Huck balances, Huck will be completely in earnest.

Throughout Mark Twain's canon, average townspeople are frequently put forth as the lowest denominator of civilization. The selfishness of small minds joins with the rigidity and hypocrisy of social acceptance, which takes the word of religion and law as stronger than the intent. Whether in the Holy Land in *Innocents Abroad* or on London Bridge in *The Prince and the Pauper,* Twain sees this spirit as mean and petty, the appropriate foil for the larger spirit of Mary Jane and Huck. It will become a mirror of Tom Sawyer's position in society in the novel's finale. In the Wilks episode, the townspeople carry on the traits established by the would-be lynch mob and the circus-goers farther up the Mississippi.

The young man who tells the king the story of the Wilks's fortune is almost too eager to reveal all the details. Twain's plan for this novel has not been to endorse local characters or local customs. The youth is "fairly emptied" by the king, Huck disgustedly reports, later calling him a "flathead." The point foreshadows the rubes who will appear to comment on and be amazed by Tom's antics at the Phelps farm later. Few people of this type fit into Twain's concept of humanitarian models until they have been elevated by some sort of education to the level of doctor, lawyer, or similar professional person.

As with the shooting of old Boggs, a crowd quickly gathers when the Duke and Dauphin first appear, but at no point does the crowd show any sense beyond vulgar curiosity. The Dauphin immediately presents himself in a maudlin and sentimental format. His expansion of Emmeline Grangerford's themes is welcomed by the crowd, and it is a member of the crowd who strikes up the "doxolojer." When the $6,000 in gold is displayed, "Everybody looked hungry at it, and licked their chops." Clearly, the crowd is as greedy as the two frauds, but lacks their guile. The doctor, a typical professional man, attacks the two frauds, describing himself as an honest friend, but "everybody" claps when the girls reject his advice in favor of "foolish friends." When the crowd approaches from the steamboat landing with an "opposition line," its boisterousness is the boisterousness of the shallowly amused—Twain's way of depicting it as uncommitted to the deeper values of protecting the girls.

When the Duke wants to leave the town without stripping the

girls of everything, the king overpowers him with a variety of arguments. The clinching argument, akin to the Duke's line, "If that don't fetch them, I don't know Arkansaw," is the Dauphin's cussing the doctor, "Hain't we got all the fools in town on our side? and ain't that a big enough majority in any town?" Here the language of majority rule—democracy—condemns democratic men. The townspeople in *Pudd'nhead Wilson* and *The Mysterious Stranger* are no better. What keeps *Huck Finn* from descending to their level of pessimism is the positioning of the king and the Duke as outsiders preying on the gullibility of the townspeople rather than as universal figures such as an "angel" Satan. The raging march to the graveyard to disinter Peter Wilks is a fitting climax to this action. It combines the violence of the lynch-mob with the inadequacy of the circus and Nonesuch audiences in a climactic scene where all the chief suspects—Duke, Dauphin, and Huck—escape. It is a heightened irony that only Huck has to account for his escape, the other two take their escape as a matter of course.

There are no analytic minds to combat the frauds. The town minister and doctor are "a-hunting," sending a sick soul to heaven; Twain the humorist removes them with a joke. When the doctor returns, his loyalty and sincerity are rejected. The lawyer and the doctor are the only townspeople who subject the competing pairs of brothers to objective analysis, the doctor by questioning their accents and the lawyer by obtaining writing samples and comparing them to letters. As Huck notes when the doctor holds his wrist, he was "plenty kind enough," but he never let go. Huck's own most compelling trait is a similar objectivity, and he regularly agrees here that any reasonable observer would follow the suspicions of the professional men. Our first vision of a rambunctious flatboatmen's democracy is being refined into a less rambunctious but more compromised village setting.

The Wilks episode as such begins with a brief reference to Providence—"meaning the devil, I reckon," says Huck—which the king trusts for a plan, but the plan is oriented toward the perversion of mannerly religion. The "orneriest old rip" looks "good and pious" as if he had just walked out of the ark or was "old Leviticus himself." Shakespeare and the Bible provide travesty reference points for the intent of the frauds. The fraudulent "*Reverend* Elexander Blodgett" changes easily into the fraudulent British clerics Harvey and William, brothers and presumed heirs of the dead Peter Wilks, when the king learns from the young rube that there is an inheritance to steal. When the greedy Duke and Dauphin revel in the gold of the Wilks girls, once again the Dauphin will lay the credit to "trust'n in Providence." Elaborating along parallel lines to the robbers on the *Walter Scott* he adds, "It's the best way in the long run. I've tried 'em all, and ther' ain't no better way." The travesty of democratic jargon on the *Walter Scott* is now also a travesty of religion used as a tool of avarice. The two will be discomfitted when they refuse to take the pile on "trust," like anyone else, find it four hundred dollars short, and put their Nonesuch profits in the bag.

The religious and quasi-religious fraud represented by the Duke and Dauphin and the oiliness of the undertaker completes Twain's travesty of the religious elements of his world and offers the dramatic contrast to Huck's private moral decision to go to hell. Twain might have thought that because these roles present travesties rather than realism he would evade criticism for attacking religion, and, in fact, he was after the universal rather than the local. When the Duke and Dauphin adopt the personae of Harvey and William Wilks and fall on each other's shoulders weeping, Huck is outspoken in terms that correspond to the ethos of the novel: "both of them took on about the dead tanner like they'd lost the twelve disciples. Well, if I ever struck anything like it, I'm a nigger. It was enough to make a body ashamed of the human race." Twain's concern with the damned human race is injected into Huck's more localized perspective to make certain that the universalism of the insight is not missed. This instance of Twain the visionary literary comedian speaking through his persona is one of the most obvious in the novel, and one of the most important, for Huck will make a similarly universalized comment when the Duke and Dauphin are tarred and feathered.

Huck continues his narrative, including phrases that suggest his disgust, as both frauds pray at the coffin, which "worked the crowd" so that women go off "sobbing and swabbing," again to Huck's open declaration that it was "disgusting." As the fraudulent speeches continue, "all full of tears and flapdoodle," Twain offers the reader a more sophisticated version of Emmeline Grangerford's bathos, now practiced for gain. As the Dauphin speaks of "holy tears" and the sore trial of missing seeing "the diseased" in life, Huck calls his proclamations, "rot and slush, till it was just sickening," capped by a "pious goody-goody Amen." Huck has never been this outspoken in the novel, and his bluntness here in the face of the fraudulently religious is remarkable.[16] Huck's yokelizing of doxology to "doxolojer" does nothing to elevate religion as a solace or even an air-freshener. When the Dauphin later says that having the fools in any town on his side is enough of a majority, his remark is already vindicated by this religion-based manipulation of the townspeople.

The chapter given over to the funeral service of the dead man further degrades religious posing through the undertaker. He is almost poetically treated, with as many sound devices expended in his portrait as in Twain's descriptions of the Mississippi River. S-alliteration is most notable; he is "softly soothering," "softest, glidingest, stealthist man I ever see," and has "no more smile than a ham," the final metaphor being the appropriately crass countrified anticlimax. When the sermon is offered, a dog begins barking and howling in the basement, and the undertaker must deal with it. His "coarse whisper" of explanation, "He had a rat," makes him the most popular man in town, as vulgar curiosity is the common town denominator. The disrupted sermon, although stories like it are common in early humor writings of Artemus Ward, especially Artemus Ward's lecture on his travels among the Mormons, is a Hartford story prominent in its day as happening to Twain's friend Reverend Joseph Twichell.[17] Localist experience could be drawn from any region for Twain just so long as it could be made to reflect on a level of mentality: thus the truly universal writer at work with his American materials.

Religion is still a negative. The hymns are played by a young woman on a sick melodium, "skreeky and colicky," again recalling Emmeline Grangerford. The funeral sermon was "pison-long and tiresome" until the funeral director closed the coffin "soft as mush," leaving Huck not knowing if the money he hid is still in the coffin. Religion here is slimy rather than violent; it is not a force to battle; it is now a lowered force to rise above. After this episode, Twain makes only a few scattered references to religion, including the story of Uncle Silas at the Phelps Farm presenting such a tremendously confused sermon that it makes his reputation for years as a deep theological thinker. Without the Roman Catholic Church to attack as in *Innocents Abroad* and *A Connecticut Yankee,* Twain has nevertheless presented religion as a tool of the deceitful and clever for cheating the stupid locals. As background for Huck's more universal battle with duty and religious punishment, it predisposes us the readers to reject religious doctrine.

The villainy in the Wilks episode is projected in terms of the gullibility of the townspeople and the greedy excesses of the king. The king's greed grows throughout the episode and is an expansion of the principle of greed seen earlier. When the greedy thieves on the *Walter Scott*, having mouthed the rhetoric of democracy, return to rob the pockets of the man they have left to die, Huck and Jim seize their boat and escape; the thieves drown. Through the Duke and the Dauphin, this same sense of punishment for greed is expanded melodramatically, climaxing finally when the Duke and Dauphin, although escaping this town, are tarred and feathered further down the river—their ultimate punishment for the Royal Nonesuch.

The whole visit is one of excesses. The excess of grief-stricken piety is typical. When they actually get Wilks's gold in their hands, the problem is slightly changed. The "boss dodge" becomes giving their own money along with the gold to the girls, expanding their fraud. The king even uses the word "rob," increasing the tension of the moment for the reader. Likewise, as the doctor accuses them of fraud, the king takes the parting shot that they will send anyone who feels sick over it to the doctor for cure. These are minor points of "hubris," however, compared to the more significant risks.

At the point when Huck has just determined to steal the money from the Duke and the king for the girls, the Duke is for taking the easy money and "lighting out," The king on the other hand sees several thousand dollars of property to be sold and the profits to be "scooped in." Ironically, the Duke says he does not want to rob a lot of orphans of "everything" they had, but the king claims first that the people who buy the items will have to give them back, and second that they are "young, and spry, and k'n easy earn a livin'." Hiding the money in a mattress and returning to their confidence game, they supply Huck with the opportunity to steal the money back for the girls.

The second instance of greed is the slave sale which underlines the humanity of family affection. Taking the opportunity of a couple of "nigger traders" passing, the king "sold them the niggers reasonable"; the slavers take the children up the river and the mother down. The word "nigger" is particularly noticeable here, and like Jim with his daughter, the slaves are presented as a family living in the town. Huck adds one more permanent memory to the stock begun when he covered the face of his murdered friend Buck Grangerford: "I can't ever get it out of my memory, the sight of them poor miserable girls and niggers hanging around each other's necks and crying." "Niggers," as so many times before, is a grating word in context, for it again confronts the reader with Huck as no more liberated from his surroundings than Twain contends he is. Huck blames the theft of the money on the slaves and the Duke criticizes the king again for "Quick sales *and* small profits." True to *his own ethic,* Huck compliments himself that he had worked the theft on the "niggers" and yet had not done them any harm by it.

At the final moment of auctioning the property, Huck comments that he had never seen "such a girafft as the king was for wanting to swallow *everything.*" Simultaneously the opposition line appears, with the crowd shouting, "you pays your money and you takes your choice." The king's fake piety and real greed, down to the last trifle, have blended together to make for his undoing.

After the escape from the Wilks embroglio, the final acts of the Duke and the king are even further degraded acts of selfishness. The Duke, at least, has some sort of insight into the process, as he admits to Huck that he and the king had come to think of Jim as theirs rather than Huck's. The conclusion, however, is that they sell Jim, fraudulently, for "forty dirty dollars." This final and ultimate greedy betrayal triggers Huck's own thoughts about Jim and leads him to his conclusion to steal Jim out of slavery. Huck broods that "after all this long journey" everything was busted up and ruined because they had the "heart" to serve Jim such a trick. The themes of the journey and gratitude and heart-knowledge emerge as Huck's response. Jim tells the story of the Royal Nonesuch, bringing on the final retributive punishment which they narrowly escaped for so long; the Duke and the Dauphin are tarred and feathered as a direct result of their betrayal of Jim.

The fourth, and most important, element in the Wilks sequence is the identification of a moral position for Huck, who must finally take sides in this episode. He comes to a series of positions which establish the groundwork for his ultimate decision to save Jim. In chapter 24, after Huck and the frauds are assigned the nicest rooms in the house, Huck is quizzed in the kitchen by Joanna, the Wilks sister with a harelip. His welcome, made uncomfortable in a burlesque sequence of questions from the harelip about his fake English life, is quickly revised by Mary Jane to be appropriate to the duties of hospitality in Catherine Beecher and Harriet Beecher Stowe's *American Woman's Home,* where visitors are to be offered the best accommodations; conversation should "express, by tone and manner, kindness and respect." The Wilks girls adhere more to the Stowes' rules than Huck, for he is fascinated by the harelip and even starts to blurt out the word, whereas they will reprimand language that would "embarrass, vex, mortify, or in any way wound the feelings of another."[18] He offers various lies and evasions, falling back on the "law" before he finally swears a false oath on a dictionary offered mistakenly as a Bible. The comic business here has some point, of course, providing one more humorous travesty of the superficiality of religion.

Following these brief emblems of the uselessness of law and religion, however, the more important action begins, for Mary Jane asserts her humane position against quizzing Huck on his stretchers as Joanna has done: "It ain't right nor kind. . . . and him a stranger . . . How would you like to be treated so?" With the reaffirmation of rightness and kindness, motifs from the raft, an alternative form of relationship is put forth again, and elaborated. Huck is a stranger and must not be shamed; he must be treated kindly—and the word "kind" appears in italics; goodness, sweetness, and loveliness are the attributes of those who show such sympathy toward a stranger.

It is as if Twain were establishing an endorsement of the Stowes' domestic philosophy, for kindness as a rule of the house will reap a large reward, although the reward comes from prevention of evil rather than an external good. As Huck apologized to Jim, so Joanna apologizes to Huck. The comic response by Huck masks the seriousness of the moment: he wishes he could tell her a thousand lies so she could apologize more. His joke is a grossly comic response to the philosophy as contained in the Stowe book. The serious response follows: Huck feels lowdown and ornery and determines to get the girls' money back for them. The girls' ethic—unquestioning kindness and the desire to give Huck a feeling of homeyness—establishes a framework for good action by him; knowing the greed of the Duke and the Dauphin, Huck plans to steal the money before his deadbeats make their getaway. The episode establishes a shore version of the relationships of the raft between Huck and Jim, but now between the girls and Huck, with Huck as the object and immediate beneficiary and respondent.

By chapter 27, the sale of the slaves has deepened the grief of Mary Jane to a point where Huck responds more actively than he originally planned. This second important chain of moral reasoning is ironic in terminology but clear in intent. Huck encounters Mary Jane weeping over the sale of the family slaves and declares impulsively that just as she can't bear to see people in trouble, he can't either, establishing again the mutuality of ethical perspectives. "Before I could think," he reassures her that the Negroes will be back in two weeks. His heart response is thus a true one separate from a studied response.

Restraining Mary Jane's anger by his concern for "another person" (Jim) and his safety, Huck must stifle his fear of the effects of reckless truth-telling:

> I says to myself, I reckon a body that ups and tells the truth when he is in a tight place, is taking considerable many resks; though I ain't had no experience. . . . I'm blest if it don't look to me like the truth is better and actuly *safer*, than a lie. . . . it's so kind of strange and unregular. . . . I'm agoing to chance it; I'll up and tell the truth this time, though it does seem most like setting down on a kag of powder and touching it off, just to see where you'll go to.[19]   (239)

Huck accepts his first great risk to carry out his moral beliefs, and reverses his comic wish to tell a thousand lies for the apologies. The risk is magnified in the metaphors, although the final punishment of lynching will become a real possibility, so the melodrama has a grounding in dramatic probabilities. Lying presumably would be recognized as a danger by nineteenth-century readers; however, in an ironic reversal, truth-telling is here described as more physically threatening. "Stretchers" have been identified as Mark Twain's habit by Huck before Joanna accused Huck of telling stretchers. In each case the idea was presented as funny; in each case the stretchers were part of a funny only partly believable masquerade, humorous verisimilitude, *not* realism. Lying about smallpox to save Jim made Huck feel like an abolitionist, here he generalizes the feeling to the dynamite metaphor; in the next few chapters he will rise to the highest moral metaphor of his culture. Ironically reversing the idea of truth-telling as an appropriate action first, he will at last have to reject one level of social truth for a higher level of personal truth, a truly existentialist dilemma.

The continuation of the events is as tightly woven as other important melodramatic sequences in the novel in the combination of burlesque elements with dramatic action. Although my analysis here takes humor first and then moves to more serious elements, Twain sets up his material in the opposite way, with more serious elements tending to come early, followed by comic matter. He does this to mute the melodrama of this section of the book, already preparing for the concluding chapters. The humor intellectualizes the action in a way that pure narrative would not be intellectualized. Readers are engaged in the literary text as an experience; were they engaged solely in the action, some sense of Huck's level of conceptualization—Mark Twain's level of conceptualization as the senior teller of stretchers and author in front of S. L. Clemens—would be missing. The work thus strengthens its character as American humor expressing American ideals by the positioning of humor around the action (the intensity of *A Connecticut Yankee* is even more obviously controlled in this way in regard to the narratives of atrocities).

Huck and Joanna end up establishing a minstrel dialogue that is like the pattern set up between Huck and Jim.[20] Before this occurs, Twain offers another passage which reemphasizes Huck's concept of lying. The apparent needlessness of the extra lie really emphasizes the necessity for philosophical management of those whose belief (southern womanly pride, here) is stronger than their drive toward results. To assure her compliance, Huck lies to Mary Jane that he will not give her "love" to the two frauds, but Twain has him pointedly state: "It was only a little thing to do, and no trouble; and it's the little things that smoothes people's roads the most, down here below; it would make Mary Jane comfortable, and it wouldn't cost nothing." Huck as pragmatist-liar is very far here from the accepted concept of truthfulness. His distortion of standards coincides comically with the pragmatism that will bring him to later decide for Jim, also the idea of comfort coincides with the ethic developed on the raft, and echoes it in light comedy.

A burlesque sequence is connected around the reasons for Mary Jane's leaving during the night. Blaming her flight on the mumps, Huck elaborates it as a many-toothed harrow of a disease named the "pluribus-unum mumps," suitably close to a patriotic phrase. Twain, with more cynicism than appears superficially, has Huck lure Joanna into silence so that she can go to England without risking quarantine. Twain evaded quarantines himself in *Innocents Abroad,* but he also wrote of disease powerfully in "Was It Heaven? Or Hell?" and *A Connecticut Yankee.* By comparison, Huck's lies about love and kisses are not as great as Joanna's projected silence about exposing others to disease in the interest of her own pleasure. Huck reemphasizes giving love and kisses immediately after and goes on to regret that he could not throw as much style into the events as Tom Sawyer. Twain thus accomplishes the triple aim of reminding the reader of Huck's level of duplicity, more active than Joanna's but on closer inspection not as bad, reechoing the earlier slave-hunters, and of foreshadowing the reentry of Tom Sawyer in chapter 33.

The quarantine business is typical of the subtle—versus the exaggerated—strain in Twain's irony. It implies that the world is made up of expanding examples of duplicitous self-serving, without adding a separate plot event. It is a deft way of suggesting a world order. Similar suggestions can be made about many other seemingly funny passages in the book which otherwise seem undirected. In fact, Huck's early remark on the widow's snuff-taking, "that was alright, because she done it herself," established the motif for this comic view of people in society as hypocrites demanding that other people live up to codes that they do not impose on themselves.

When a character like Colonel Sherburn bursts through this pretense, his actions are melodramatic confrontations of the crowd. As Huck will soon burst through the pretense melodramatically, his action is polarized around this same division: what is expected versus what feels better personally. The effect of the passage with Joanna is to establish the subtlest overtone that Huck, although he acts alone, represents more than himself. It frees the reader to sympathize with him and the good motivation he has; Huck's intent is much superior to the selfish motivations causing others to ignore laws and rules of society, even though *they* are accepted within their villages while he is not.

The high point of the chapter is one of the most important endorsements of Huck in the book. Unable to see her crying while "them devils" lay under her roof "shaming and robbing her," Huck reveals the truth about the Duke and the Dauphin to Mary Jane. Berating himself for losing the $6,000 in gold in the coffin of Peter Wilks, Huck is told by Mary Jane to stop blaming himself. At the final moment of leaving, Mary Jane says she will think of Huck "many and many a time" and *pray* for him as well. Huck then offers one of his most heartfelt soliloquies. He exclaims that she would pray for Judas if she took a notion to, for there was "no back-down to her." Thus, Huck allies himself with the greatest betrayer in the Christian faith—next to Satan himself, whom Huck referred to a scant three lines earlier in describing the Duke and Dauphin as "them devils." Huck's speech builds the moment by reasserting Mary Jane's grit, and he mentions also her beauty and goodness. He concludes by restating her willingness to pray for him, weighted with repetitions to emphasize the emotional importance to Huck, and seeming to distance the event in time: "I hain't ever seen her since that time I see her go out of that door; no, I hain't ever seen her since; but I reckon I've thought of her a many and a many a million times, and of her saying she would pray for me; and if ever I'd a thought it would do any good for me to pray for *her*, blamed if I wouldn't a done it or bust." Huck here has been endorsed by and has endorsed a person from the riverbank culture. Religion, taken seriously, has provided him with the medium. Twain demonstrates through Huck's feelings that it is not the raft and river as such but the relationships between people which elevate human sympathy. As he responds to Jim, so Huck responds to Mary Jane and she to him; they measure and respect each other in relation to their *kindness* to each other, and they are ready to take each other at face value.

Victor Doyno (in an essay in *One Hundred Years of Huckleberry Finn*), after studying the original manuscript, noted that Twain deleted a number of words that suggested a sexual attraction between Huck and Mary Jane. Twain is seeking to project the fullest picture of the natural humanity of kindliness, his contribution to the defense of the individual against corporate society, corporate morality, and corporate commonness of man. Recognizing that this visionary democratic message would only be blunted by the confusion of sexuality with the higher level of intimacy implied in this marriage of true minds, Twain revised the language of the Huck-Mary Jane scenes. The crucial common denominator is kindness; Huck's strongest feelings towards the girls were a result of kindness, and his greatest expressed aversion to the Duke and Dauphin was that they took advantage of the girls' kindness to shame and rob them. Huck's original acceptance of the Duke and Dauphin on the raft was based on the premise that everyone should feel right and kind toward the others. The principle has now been established as a central one throughout Huck and Jim's dealings and a means for charting new and more moral courses.

– 9 –

Huck's Moral Reasoning
as Heroism

The climax of the novel, the point at which it becomes truly an American classic, is Huck's decision to go to hell to save Jim in chapter 31. The action from chapter 29—the wrapping up of the Wilks episode—through chapters 30 and 31 leads directly to this climax. Huck's "Judas" speech foreshadows it, and after this point, Huck is largely helpless in relation to events, even though they are events which he set in motion. Tom Sawyer's reentry into the novel will bring finality to Huck's diminished power in normal society. Huck is passive in the actions of chapters 29 and 30, as events outpace his plans. Nonetheless, Providence is developed in the action in a way that suggests belief, not skepticism, and the Wilks episode concludes with its climactic acknowledgment by Mary Jane and the recapture of the raft by the Duke and Dauphin. All that remains is the full coming to moral manhood by Huck. He does so in terms which are consistent with a Victorian vision of morality, suggesting the superficiality of the reading given *Adventures of Huckleberry Finn* by its critics in Concord. *The Royal Path of Life* is one of many sources that give a contemporary basis for the nature of Huck's decision, and study of that manual of social life throws light on Huck's radicalism. Twain, himself, never fully reconciled his ideas with this solution, and it ultimately became the pessimism of *What Is Man?*

Upon the appearance of the "opposition line," the Duke and Dauphin's fortunes lead, naturally, to their eventual tar and feathering. Late in chapter 29 Huck is complimented by Levi Bell the lawyer as being pretty awkward at lying; a natural outcome of the situation, the comment is suggestive of the reversals surrounding Huck. A lynch mob forms around the pairs of Wilks claimants. Business about the tattoo on the dead man's chest takes the entire town to the graveyard for a melodramatic disinterment during an oncoming thunderstorm, and the crescendo of events provides the climax for Huck's involvement with the Duke and Dauphin. Huck escapes as the townspeople lunge forward—as we know crowds do from the Boggs-Sherburn incident—to look at the spectacle of the gold on the dead man's chest.

Huck's escape embodies emotional climaxes built on three important elements. First, as he runs through the darkened and deserted town, he sees the light go on in Mary Jane's window, meaning that she has returned as agreed to help Huck. He is rescued from feeling "sorry and disappointed" and his heart "swelled up sudden, like to bust," with the same rapidity as the steamboat that overran the raft, "and the same second the house and all was behind me in the dark, and wasn't ever going to be before me no more in this world." Huck is talking in the language of ultimates, even though the action need not be ultimate; a sense of absolute finality surrounds Huck's moral actions. Second, Huck returns to the raft, is knocked overboard by the sight of Jim as King Leer (*sic*) and a drownded A-rab, and they flee: "It *did* seem so good to be free again and all by ourselves on the big river and nobody to bother us." The theme of the river and freedom and security from society is reechoed only to be destroyed in the third important component of this passage; the Duke and the Dauphin are heard rowing across the river and Huck "wilted right down onto the planks, then, and give up." This series of turns and reversals provides us with a climax reestablishing Huck and Jim, but within a paragraph sweeps away our relief, in a tragic reinvasion by the mock royalty, grown more like Pap Finn. The usurpers have gained their freedom, and Jim and Huck and the raft are recaptured. The king even begins to shake Huck and threatens to drown him, placing him essentially in the same jeopardy that caused him to flee from Pap Finn. Important themes of security, kindness, and resolution are mingled in the concluding defeat for Huck and Jim. By the end of the chapter, the two rapscallions lie drunkenly and lovingly in each other's arms, "as thick as thieves again," while Huck and Jim are reduced to the level of auxiliaries.

Chapter 31 is a purposefully weakened return to the river in which Twain shows the two thieves falling back on their shallow resources, faking dancing schools and yellocution lessons with the facility of Artemus Ward's pet kangaroo—a standing joke of the literary comedian Ward in the 1860s for the fraudulent representation of moral and uplifting entertainment, based on Barnum's Museum. Huck is at his most dryly Twain-like distance from the two rogues as the raft journey continues. A lowered level of intensity from the events of the Wilks episode corresponds to the conspiratorial whisperings of the Duke and Dauphin in the wigwam. When the Duke and Huck discover the king drunk in a village "doggery," Huck flees to the raft and finds that Jim has vanished. For the second time in this part of the novel, Huck talks of crying, and this time actually does—he only does so twice in the novel. He will shortly learn that Jim is at the Silas Phelps farm twelve miles down the river, sold as an escaped slave by the king for the money to get drunk on. Huck will then encounter the Duke and give him ten cents, as he had done with his own Pap before—echoing that relationship from the early part of the novel—and pretend to strike for the back country. The actual effort to free Jim will be the anticlimax to the moral climax of the novel which occurs in this chapter.

Huck's moral decision proceeds by reversals and contrasts when Huck sits down in the wigwam on the raft to think—which he does until he wears his head sore. His reasoning is based, as in the Wilks episode, on loyalty through kindness. He criticizes the Duke and the Dauphin "after all this long journey, and after all we'd done for them . . . all come to nothing" because they had the "heart" to trick Jim and "make him a slave again all his life, and amongst strangers, too, for forty dirty dollars." The Duke and the Dauphin, of course, were just as eager to sell the Wilks slaves to strangers, so this particular level of unfeeling is characteristic of them. However, Mary Jane and her sisters and Huck have all had in common the regard for slaves being kept among their own people. Perhaps more compelling is the idea of the forty dirty dollars, close enough to the thirty pieces of silver of Judas's betrayal of Christ to carry that resonance of cosmic ugliness of spirit. Huck's thinking in this paragraph is a summary of everything that the Duke and the Dauphin demonstrated in relation to the Wilks girls, but here it has come home to himself and Jim. He had already combatted their actions once; now his problem will be to combat them at a still larger level of action which he will have to reason out through the tortuous reversals of ethics which Miss Watson's Christianity imposes on his purer and simpler "sound heart but deformed conscience."

For all the melodramatic excitement of the events of the novel up to this point, the greatest event of the book takes place as Huck's internal monologue; the monologue represents one of the truly great moments in American fiction. The moment had as much importance to the readers of 1885 as it retains for modern critics, perhaps even more. To suggest the nature of Huck's courage as a Victorian ideal, we might refer to a moral self-instructor, such as *The Royal Path of Life,* subtitled "Aims and Aids to Success and Happiness," written by T. L. Haines, A. M., and L. W. Yaggy, M. S.[21] It has not been demonstrated that Twain owned or read this particular volume, but it is so representative of a variety of such books that embodied the ethics of his generation of Americans that it provides a vital touchstone for his and his readers' emotional demands on Huck if Huck is to rise to true greatness in representing their highest ethical impulses. *The Royal Path's* statements on "Courage" describe fully Huck Finn's ultimate heroism within the life of the book. First, we must accept Huck's realistically portrayed world as one of small rather than noble actions—a point consistent not only with literary realists, but also with pragmatic moralists and, at the plot level, for those readers already disliking Tom Sawyer's style.

The Royal Path states: "To lead the forlorn hope in the field of courage requires less nerve than to fight nobly and unshrinkingly the bloodless battle of life. To bear evil speaking and illiterate judgement with equanimity, is the highest bravery. It is in fact the repose of mental courage" (216). Huck is the self-effacing hero of this ideal. As well, the quotation describes the Duke and the Dauphin's relation to Huck, for their Shakespeare demonstrated their lack of literate judgment, only superseded by the lowness of those they cheated. Huck's tears were for despair over Jim; his manner has indeed been to fight the "bloodless" battles—and at present, he has lost, for Jim has been taken back into slavery far from home. *The Royal Path* elaborates: "Physical courage, which despises all danger, will make a man brave in one way; and moral courage, which despises all opinion, will make a man brave in another. The former would seem most necessary for the camp, the latter for council; but to constitute a great man, both are necessary" (216). Huck has just endured physical danger—the threats of a lynch mob—while attempting to bring forth good for Mary Jane in secret. His courage has been suggested by the ultimate terms he uses in treating his relationship to her. The moral courage which despises all opinion is suggested by the fact that only she knew of his goodness, a powerful foreshadowing of his further seeking in private for Jim's good. Huck abandoned interests he might have had in aiding the Duke and Dauphin, thus becoming irrelevant to them. Twain had already used Colonel Sherburn to disparage the courage of men in an army. Thus most of the elements of the textbook definition of personal courage are played out before the reader's eyes.

The Royal Path continues in the same vein:

> No one can tell who the heroes are, and who the cowards, until some crisis comes to put us to the test. And no crisis puts us to the test that does not bring us up alone and single-handed to face danger. It is nothing to make a rush with the multitude even into the jaws of destruction. Sheep will do that. Armies might be picked from the gutter, and marched up to make food for powder. But when some crisis singles one out from the multitude, pointing at him the particular finger of fate, and telling him, "Stand or run," and he faces about with steady nerve, with nobody else to stand behind, we may be sure the hero stuff is in him. When such a crisis comes, the true courage is just as likely to be found in people of shrinking nerves, or in weak and timid women, as in great burly people. It is a moral, not a physical trait. . . . A good cause makes a courageous heart. . . . Though the occasions of high heroic daring seldom occur but in the history of the great, the less obtrusive opportunities for the exertion of private energy are continually offering themselves. With these, domestic scenes as much abound as does the tented field. . . . It rescues the unhappy from degradation, and the feeble from contempt. (216–17)

Huck is a low rather than a heroic figure. His setting is domestic, especially as developed in the Wilks episode, rather than chivalric. Most important, he and Jim have been the powerless feeble in the face of the authority of Duke and Dauphin and townspeople, alike, as demonstrated by the recapture of the raft by royalty and of Jim by the local bounty-seekers. The ethic proposed is romantic democracy at its highest, relying on the individual, no matter how low; true to the beliefs of the founding fathers, as well, it distrusts collective man as a mob. In fact, it embodies the dominant formative beliefs of American culture as opposed to the beliefs of communist and collectivist cultures even today.

Huck's Moral Reasoning as Heroism

Six paragraphs comprise Huck's highest moral statement, climaxing in his decision to "steal Jim out of slavery again," and if he can think of anything worse to "go the whole hog." Huck begins by considering the disgust of people toward himself and Jim for trying to escape. He advances to his sense of Providence punishing him, and continues to seek help in prayer and in a letter to Miss Watson to free himself from "sin." Reminiscences of the raft journey lead to personalizing rather than moralizing, and he reverses his plan of action and decides to follow out Jim's wishes and his own human sense of feeling the true "right" thing, rather than the demands of his conscience.

Huck thus sits down to think, not on the tented field but in the wigwam of the raft. He cannot write to Tom Sawyer because Miss Watson will be disgusted at Jim's "rascality and ungratefullness" and sell him down the river again. As readers, we have no difficulty in detecting this obvious irony of the naif. Crushingly, as with any government, the worst punishment comes for trying to rebel, and it comes by guaranteeing the event that caused the rebellion. Selfishness from Huck, as with Joanna, also figures in this level of the reasoning. Huck protests the disgrace falling on "*Me!*" for helping "a nigger to get his freedom." The emphasis on slavery and freedom is such that no reasonable reader could help developing allegiance with the other side of Huck's reasoning, as yet not emerged. The word "freedom," in fact, puts the reader emotionally ahead of Huck in the reasoning process.

The ironic reversals of moral purpose continue in the most intense passages in the novel. Huck has just noted how heartless it was for the Duke and Dauphin to betray Jim. Consequently, the reader is immediately prepared for Huck's reasoning as he, in his own turn, considers the betrayal of Jim, either for Jim's own good or for Huck's good through conscience-cleansing. As prepared for in the Wilks episode, the turn to microcosmic personal experience is a crucial determiner of moral action. As Huck sees "Jim before me, all the time, in the day, and in the night-time," he conjures up a brief history of the warmest moments of the protectiveness of Jim. In opposition to the loneliness of his room at the widow's or in the face of even his admired leader Tom, Huck remembers "we a floating along, talking, and singing, and laughing." Huck cannot "strike no places to harden me against him." The hardness of feeling versus its opposite kindness becomes the means by which Twain allows the heart to overcome the conscience. Huck even gives the reader a reprise of events: Jim standing watch, the fog, the feud and the swamp reconciliation, Huck's lie about the small-pox when Jim called Huck his "best friend old Jim ever had in the world, and the *only* one he's got now." The language of this last sentence is again the language of ultimates—the world, the isolation of the two in their joined purpose. It is language which establishes the basis for Huck's response at an equally ultimate and universal level.

Huck's rightness of heart is also equated to religion by Twain, establishing the antimoral antagonist to personal goodness: abstract moral training. Abstract ideology identified Jim as an "ungrateful nigger." Huck feels boot-licking shame from hiding the disgrace of doing a "low-down thing." Notably, Twain does not name Huck's specific sin other than "to help a nigger get his freedom." As Huck studies the matter, "my conscience went to grinding me." Finally, Huck comes to the ultimate moral abstraction and declares that "the plain hand of Providence" is slapping him for his "wickedness." The crime is now specified: "stealing a poor old woman's nigger that hadn't ever done me no harm." Twain is at his best in using dramatic irony here; each term of Huck's self-reproach is intuitively—subconsciously and consciously—felt by readers to be false. Miss Watson was not a poor old woman, she was a lean old maid with goggles on. She was not someone who never harmed Huck; first, she made him feel lonely and restricted; second, she initiated the dispatch of Huck to hellfire, even sending Tom with him. *We*, the readers, know that Huck is reasoning a wrong position. When the "One" scares Huck and Huck confronts himself with going to Sunday school, readers of *Tom Sawyer* will remember the fraudulent collection of Bible study tickets; readers of *Huck Finn* will review the scepticism toward Sunday school in the early part of the book and the travesty of religion portrayed in the Grangerford feud.

Huck's attempt to "pray a lie" is given its own paragraph. It demonstrates again the emotional mystification that corrupt social religion has worked on Huck. Why can't he pray, Huck asks himself—and answers, because "my heart warn't right." Huck's heart is committed by daily life to Jim and to the events that have made the raft seem its own separate world; his heart is more involved and refined than those of the Duke and Dauphin. All the reverse morality of Pap Finn and the robbers on the *Walter Scott*, and all the implications of Jim stealing his own family from their rightful owners, and all the implications of Huck offending against the people of his hometown by stealing a "poor old woman's nigger" lie behind the dramatic irony of this confusion worked on natural instinct by social precept. The passage taps into the deepest concerns of civilized man—the perception of self in relation to moral action.

Huck's Moral Reasoning as Heroism

Twain appeals not only to our concepts as observers of society through literature, and not only to our satisfaction with the working out of image and form in the literary work; here he appeals also to the needy child in all readers hidden behind the coolly self-denying façade of adulthood.[22] Huck's debate with himself exemplifies Twain's contention that he showed a boy with a sound heart but a deformed conscience working out the problems of life. Huck's recognition that only his mouth is saying he will do the "right thing," ironically reversed, triggers in readers an enthusiasm for reversal; the reversal of Huck's saying that he wished he would go to hell to Miss Watson has already established the basis for its repetition and expansion to a wider moral field of action. Another deft abstraction by Twain has Huck refer to writing to "that nigger's owner." Naming a legal entity rather than a person reemphasizes the tension between an individual's feelings and social-legal rights. When Huck says that "He knowed it,"—God knows he is lying—the cosmic irony of his dilemma is complete.

It is not clear that God has taken the opposite side, of course, only that he sees Huck's actions; it is Huck who imputes evil to himself. Huck writes a note to Miss Watson and then feels himself "washed clean of sin for the first time I had ever felt so in my life." Where this statement might have a positive power, the camp meeting sequence has undercut this sort of ideology already. Huck's good feeling is held for a moment with no reason given—and none is needed other than the reader's demand for a resolution to the ironic constraints that baffle satisfaction—and then Huck "went on thinking." His thinking is composed of the last great reprise of the raft journey, with each of the moments on board designated as a happy one filled with immediate personal love demonstrated through affection. All the emotions of loneliness overcome and violence escaped from—the negative force of the book—and all the building up of personal affection between Huck and Jim—as fully activated in Huck's responsive aid to Mary Jane Wilks—the positive force of the book—focus in the most intense moment of the novel. Huck, leaping again to the language of ultimates proclaims, "It was a close place. . . . I was a trembling because I'd got to decide, forever, betwixt two things and I knowed it." Huck decides to go to hell; Huck decides in favor of the will to freedom by his friend Jim.

Huck's decision to go to hell is his greatest moment. It confirms the reader's rejection of the irony which Twain has created. It has the power of Ahab's rejection of heaven, even though the "tore it up" completing action is minuscule. The particularity of the moment and its privacy is the fulfillment of the ultimate act of moral heroism as identified in *The Royal Path*. In the realist's world of social, political, and industrial might, the turn to private individual action is the response of the isolated man. Huck's finest hour has with it the futility of its individuality. Endorsed as it is by the textbook moralists of *The Royal Path*, it is not the ethic of power. Couched in the language of self-denial—the truly Christian sense of sinful unworthiness—Huck's planning establishes an underlayer of acceptance in his choice for the later submission to Tom Sawyer which some critics find so perplexing. Yet this psychoreligious level of the novel's action as fully supports Tom Sawyer's reentry as does Huck's repeated wishing that he could have carried out Tom Sawyer effects to complete several plot events.

Huck's abandonment of the idea of reform fulfills his decision to go to hell and also foreshadows his relinquishing of power to Tom. He declares that he will take up wickedness, separating himself from Tom and others in society, even though he had also been happy to hear Miss Watson say that Tom would go to hell. The language of ethics has become the ironic language of the character's own moral reasoning. His upbringing is part of thinking, and as Miss Watson and Pap were primary landmarks in that experience, some further denial of that upbringing is in order. His declaration that he would not only steal Jim out of slavery satisfies the demands of readers—Nook Farmers and all—that slavery be denied as an evil. Huck's determination to go "whole hog" even reechoes the commentary on hogs going to church and the maltreatment of hogs in the river town of Bricksville. Huck's ultimate choice is a choice of hoggishness as complete in its individualization as Pap's drunkenness—his was the hand of a hog, after all—but with such an incalculably higher object that readers must thrill in response to the final irony, as deftly sophisticated as any reflected image in American fiction. It is small wonder that, despite its importance, analytic readers feel restive during the conclusion of the novel which follows, comprising almost a fifth of the book's length.

Twain's optimism manifests itself in Huck Finn's action. In a private act of conscience, a person's kindness responds to kindness and guarantees ultimate human rights. For Twain, this truth is the highest law. Trowbridge, in *Cudjo's Cave* in a somewhat different context, had established the same hierarchy of values. He has a young German-American lad, Carl, refuse to honor a contract with a slaveholder, only to be reassured by the blind minister Mr. Villiers that "sometimes people do wrong from a motive so pure and disinterested that it sanctifies the action" (206). American culture had the moral machinery in place as fiction for twenty years by the time Huck Finn took his stand on the front porches of Twain's subscribers. Later, in *What Is Man?* (1906), Twain gave a more pessimistic view of the same kind of action. Contemplating Hamilton's duel with Burr, he proposes that Hamilton was driven by "public standards of honor." He continues that when standards of "love" seem to apply, however, they merely serve "to secure his personal comfort." Huck's thinking does indeed coincide with this model. Conscience is a thing which twists in order to gratify self-approval in both Huck's case and in Twain's later pessimism. The moment is elevated in *Huckleberry Finn* by its focus on the good outcome, parallel with the democratic philosophy. Late in his life, Twain withdrew from that external solace.

In a number of ways the novel seems to end here. The Duke and Huck are finally separated with Huck performing an act like he had performed with his own Pap, giving the Duke ten cents. The Duke, starting to tell the truth, reverses himself and lies to Huck, thus completing their separation. He went to "studying," just as Tom will do shortly in betraying Huck and Jim to his own fantasy fun. The Duke, part way between a feeling of sympathy and a threateningly "ugly" look of violence, in effect plays into Huck's plan by threatening Huck and sending him away. The chapter closes, in the original edition, with a picture of the back of Huck as he heads into the country—the perfect visual statement for an ending.

However, Huck has plans to get shut of that kind. He will further his own general plan at the Phelps farm, finally concluding his adventures with Tom and Jim. The great moral decision has been made, however. The moral triumph of the raft ethic is complete in terms of the great river. Now, it will be transmuted and diminished to the reality of the shore—and of Twain's realistic view of society.

$-$ 10 $-$

The Last Fifth of the Novel as Echo: The Phelps Farm

The last fifth of *Huck Finn,* chapters 31 through 43, although they have been a problem for analytic critics, have been less a problem for general readers. To general readers, the chapters flow out of the continuing events of the trip. The picaresque narrative gives no particular means of identifying any change in the nature or "level" of action. Nor has Huck's motivation changed. It has matured with his "go to hell" speech into an announced purpose, but this purpose does not allow for a diminishing of the importance of his actions, just the opposite. He is now committed to freeing Jim at any cost. The events that follow, including the extended burlesque of chivalric literature in Tom's participation, might well be regarded as a continuing expansion of the themes of the novel, adding to rather than detracting from the reader's final understanding of Huck and the reader's sharing of his experience.

The last fifth of *Huck Finn* actually takes place only because Huck decided to go to hell. Had he written home to Miss Watson, doing the "right" thing, the journey would end with him giving up Jim's freedom and, more important, giving up his commitment to Jim the person over his commitment to social custom and religious law. For Huck the issue is simple, and it is an issue that Twain wrote on again in such stories as "Was it Heaven? Or Hell?" Should one's own soul be preserved by rigid adherence to religious codes, or is kindness toward other people the primary saving grace? In Twain's stories, his heroes consistently choose the second course. Truly American is Twain the comedian on the same issue: having disposed of it through private personal introspection true to the Puritan tradition and *The Royal Path*, he now goes on to joke about it. Huck's brilliant leap beyond moral law subjects him to chaotic events—mostly manipulated by Tom Sawyer, freed by his knowledge of Jim's real status to make a game out of that which is serious to Huck and Jim. The irony of Jim's already achieved freedom is that Huck is not an outlaw. For Twain to offer a realistic portrayal of antisocial action, in fact, might have been a greater problem. As critics, we must remember that Jim is already free unbeknownst to us and Huck; we as readers thus worry less about the futility of Huck and Jim being ridiculous. Tom Sawyer will externalize that ridiculousness in the plot. Reechoing themes already posed in the first seven chapters of the novel, the ending successfully and even powerfully brings together the themes of St. Petersburg and disposes of them, giving Huck's concluding line in the novel its importance. In Huck's case, neither social acceptance nor rebellion guarantees that his actions will be meaningful—his success, by the terms of the end of the novel, becomes solely one of the spirit, especially one of the American spirit blazing its own new moral path.

Huck has only a brief time at the Phelps farm before Tom Sawyer reenters, but in that time the reader is reoriented to the emotions conveyed through Huck's life at St. Petersburg. Huck arriving at the farm describes the identical feelings which he had after Miss Watson had worked on him. The farm is Sunday-like, lonesome, mournful, "like everybody's dead and gone," and makes Huck wish he was dead, too. After a deft genre painting of the Arkansas plantation, Huck reiterates his wish that he was dead as he listens to the mournful sound of a spinning wheel. Although Huck has just decided to go to hell, he again puts his trust in Providence to give him a plan of action, "for I'd noticed that Providence always did put the right words in my mouth, if I left it alone." Twain thus ignores Huck's self-damnation, so secure is he as author in the flow of the narrative, to place Huck again under superior divine protection, to suggest his helplessness, and to identify him once again as a saddened victim of emotions appropriate to his condition as a stranger or outsider.

Actually, Huck's greeting is a warm one. Aunt Sally Phelps hugs him, hides him briefly to play a trick on Uncle Silas—establishing playing tricks as something that can be innocently done to one another's loved ones—and finally reveals, to Huck as well as Uncle Silas, that he is "Tom Sawyer," for whom he has been mistaken. The kindly

Uncle Silas responds directly with honest enthusiasm in his greeting, and Huck declares that it is like being born again, a situation appropriate to the climax of the novel. Since Huck has almost told the truth, recalling that major displacement of his premises, this little episode replays the major components of the Wilks episode. Within this setting, like a gem of purest ray serene, lies Huck's explanation of the delay of his supposed steamboat transportation:

> "It warn't the grounding—that didn't keep us back but a little. We blowed out a cylinder head."
>> "Good gracious, anybody hurt?"
>> "No'm. Killed a nigger." (279)

The implication of the passage is so succinct that clinching it with a further line as Twain does is almost unnecessary: "Well, it's lucky, because sometimes people do get hurt." A paragraph of literary comedy follows, including one of the century's most widely used anticlimaxes, a relative "turned blue all over, and died in the hope of a glorious resurrection." The purpose is plainly to identify callousness to blacks as a social constant, with overtones of comic stupidity. In concept, the status of "niggers" has not changed for a typical Arkansas farm woman, no matter what experience Huck has gone through. Lying to disguise himself in this society, Huck shows the offhandedness of the planters of the region as depicted in such narratives as J. T. Trowbridge's *A Picture of the Desolated States and the Work of Restoration, 1865–1868*. As noted previously, Trowbridge often uses the term "nigger," but it occurs only within quoted speech to characterize the antagonistic attitudes of the region as embodied in its language. Nor would Twain use such an epithet anywhere outside of his fictional language. If some black readers feel a sense of outrage at these lines, they are correctly responding to Twain's intent after Huck's climactic decision, although some of them may miss his purposefulness in achieving their response. For Twain, the literary comedy of the following passage completes the suggestion of silliness attached to Aunt Sally as the victim of Huck's disguise. It only remains for Huck to meet and merge forces with the real Tom Sawyer to complete the foundation for the last fifth of the book.

Tom and Huck rejoin almost immediately. Huck connives to meet Tom and convinces Tom that he is not dead: "I hain't come back—I hain't been *gone!*" But he is surprised when Tom agrees, after "studying"—usually an indication of selfish planning in Twain's romantic view of human action—to become with Huck a "nigger stealer." Tom also treats his reentry into the scene with "an amount of style that was suitable," coming like the ram rather than the sheep, in Huck's suggestive barnyard metaphor. But even here, every reference manages a comic negativity: a stranger is more interesting than the yellow fever; Uncle Silas's preaching for free is worth it. The cap is Tom's kissing Aunt Sally and arousing wrath only to quell it with one of his revelations of innocence. Foreshadowing later and larger dangers, Tom says that his kissing was a mistake—"This ain't no healthy place for a stranger to come"—although Tom's joke is revealed and all is forgiven by the relieved adults. In short, he plays out the "Evasion" pattern that he will next create at length as Jim's fraudulent escape. Huck, true to the pattern, next describes dinner as not tasting like a hunk of old cold cannibal—a Twainism of literary humor rather than a natural Huck metaphor. Echoing the life of the first three chapters, Huck comments that Uncle Silas's prayers over it did not spoil it. Nor, in fact, will Tom's appropriation of Huck and Jim's adventure spoil them, either.

One anomaly that Twain has to clear up is Tom's willingness to engage in a genuinely antisocial act. Readers of *The Adventures of Tom Sawyer* have already seen him pretend death, distressing his family, not to mention humiliating schoolmasters and fooling friends, but each of these egocentricities allowed later forgiveness and social acceptance. Huck confronts the issue head-on in chapter 34. He wonders, making explicit for us his own freedom, how a well-brought-up boy like Tom Sawyer could "steal the nigger." The words used are "respectable," "well brung up," "pride," "rightness," and "feeling." Where these words might ally Tom with people like the Grangerfords and Miss Watson, other phrases would equally ally him with the professional level of society, as represented by Dr. Robinson in the Wilks episode for example: "bright and not leatherheaded," and "not mean, but kind." Tom strongly asserts that he knows what he is doing, and Huck "just let it go." Tom's rudeness and covertness may distance him from us as readers more than Huck's do, establishing a basis for our allegiance to Huck even while we enjoy Tom's travesties of escape romances. With that letting go, Huck and the reader assign responsibility for the coming action to Tom's "new bullinesses," up to fifteen-fold more stylish than Huck's simple escape plan, "and maybe get us all killed, besides." The ironic divergence from Huck's mode leads to the next six chapters of highly intellectualized burlesque. Tom's socially acceptable outlawry has comic potential, and Huck's sense of its real potential is moved to the level of irony. In part, at least, Huck's irony is a major component of Twain's understanding of and picture of his world; for Tom, the fun will be "intellectual."

A second foundation is laid down for the conclusion as the final lines are written to the story of the Duke and Dauphin. Huck had left the Duke hanging posters for his Royal Nonesuch routine, and the matter of the Negro "blowing" on them had already been threatened. Huck had planned to silence Jim to provide for a final separation. Thus, a culmination of the rascals' relationship to Jim and Huck is heavily foreshadowed. Tom and Huck, learning at supper that Jim has indeed told the story, are too late to prevent disaster. As with earlier lynch mobs, this mob, carrying the tarred and feathered Duke and Dauphin on a rail, comes with a "raging rush of people," with torches and yelling and other indicators of social chaos. Huck's declaration to us the readers—not to an Aunt Sally for social effect but to us in soliloquy—projects the purified sympathy appropriate to the "raft-voyage" he has just described to Tom. Seeing them as looking like nothing in the world that was human, Huck calls them "poor pitiful rascals" and says he cannot feel any hardness toward them again "in the world": "It was a dreadful thing to see. Human beings can be awful cruel to one another." Huck's language is again the language of universals. This comment, together with Huck's lie about the steamboat delay, reemphasizes that the novel has really staked out kindness toward human beings—the humanization of all human beings—as its driving motive. Indifference to suffering, by dehumanizing a black, or the conscious working of suffering, even as punishment, on a white, is equally objectionable to readers sensitized by Huck's reasoning about both Jim and the Duke and the Dauphin. To see the novel as solely about Huck's relation to Jim is to narrow the full dimensions of its humanity.

Huck's final comment on conscience concludes the chapter. He says that he and Tom felt low down, ornery, and "humble," a suggestively religious word perhaps. Huck and Tom share the guilt of the act, even though they had not perpetrated it. Huck says a person's conscience ain't got no sense and just goes for him anyway—it ain't no good, takes up too much room, and should be poisoned like a "yaller dog." This final comment on conscience expresses the pessimism of later Twainian writings: "A man will do ANYTHING, no matter what it is, *to secure his spiritual comfort.*"[23] Twain had argued that most men's actions were controlled by the approval of neighbors and society. He had also suggested that the "inborn necessity of contenting his own spirit" controlled everything a man does. Huck and Tom's reasoning on conscience is a noncommital indication of the same possibility. Since Huck has already abandoned his conscience for a higher inborn command, however, this persistence of conscience is somewhat duplicitous on Twain's part. He manages to have Huck and Tom be at once moral and immoral, an ambiguity which is built into Huck's lying from the very first. So, as the Duke and the Dauphin leave the scene, they leave the hero feeling as if he had failed in his humanitarian duty. This universalist Christian position of responsibility to all—and of innate guilt—is worthy of Miss Watson's doctrine, although Miss Watson is more self-aggrandizing. In the broadest sense, Huck has failed for all of his own great leap to social independence and moral dependence on his friend to make the leap for others. The stage is perfectly set for Tom Sawyer to take control of the action, and Huck's lack of power in the world is already identified for us.

Literary comedy is more obvious throughout the final chapters. Huck's irony in the pages introducing the Phelps farm shows one-liner jokes and anticlimaxes. Tom likewise carries out a lengthier prank typical of his own, rather than Huck's, "adventures." The merging of the seriousness of Huck's enterprise with the burlesque of Tom's allows for the earned reentry of Huck and Jim into the "real" world of local society. Tom's "Why Jim is—"response to Huck's announcement that he will steal Jim out of slavery leads to our guess that Jim is, in fact, free, and the force of his predicament is thus altered. Certainly some part of the reader's mind must be aware from Tom's cut-off sentence that something is radically wrong with the premises now governing the external action.

The conclusion of the novel follows in three major units: first, Tom's romantic contriving versus Huck's pragmatism in freeing Jim; second, the yokel posse and the shooting of Tom, with Jim's recapture; and finally, the concluding revelations. The first sequence is Twain's greatest travesty of literary romance prior to *A Connecticut Yankee,* the book that alienated so many medieval sentimentalists among his British readership in 1889. The second sequence provides a readaptation of Huck and Jim to their world. The third allows Huck his final freedom, and introduces the line which more than any other summarizes the nature of his whole experience.

S. B. Liljegren in *The Revolt Against Romanticism in the Works of S. L. Clemens* (New York: Haskell House, 1970 [1945]) has noted how the travesty for Twain represented an attack on the falsified sentiment of the romantics. All of Tom's activities from chapter 34 through 40 are travesties. Against them are set the modest refusals of Huck, and physical consequences—usually comic—for all three participants: Huck, Jim, and Tom. The objections of the pragmatic Huck are the sole explicit evidence of Twain's revolt against romanticism. All else is expressed through the exaggerated action where the security of Tom's socially acceptable troublemaking allows a vast array of slapstick activities. They take on meaning, however, by testing the philosophy of Jim and Huck and allowing them to replay their sensitivity away from the raft. Imprisoned in Tom's absurdity, their feelings are trivialized to the same extent that the feelings of any character in later existentialist drama are trivialized. An ironic realism similar to that which causes the word "nigger" to appear so frequently also causes Jim and Huck's subordination in these chapters. The simplicity with which Twain elaborates on the final punishment of the Duke and Dauphin makes a touching comparison to Tom's elaborations. Set just after Tom's psychological trick on Aunt Sally and *just before* his romantic contrivances, it predetermines the reader to mistrust elaborate device. When Huck acts, even unsuccessfully as here, important events are handled simply and with dispatch; but when Tom acts, events are marked by needless delay and involvement. Twain himself predisposes the reader not to like what Tom is doing—of course.

Much of the irony of this section is overt. For example, in identifying Jim's location, Tom observes a watermelon being taken into a locked shed, identifying a prisoner—and there couldn't be two such prisoners "where the people's all so kind and good." That there should be a prisoner there at all, let alone one whom Tom knows is a free man, is ironic. With Huck it is similar. Huck is, in response to Tom's romance, still the pragmatist. His plan is to steal Uncle Silas's key, unlock Jim, and raft down the river at night; even Tom admits the plan would work, but he rejects it because it wouldn't make enough talk. Tom's criteria, including their own contradictions, are that a plan be "mysterious, and troublesome, and good."

The early chapters of the novel are reechoed thoroughly. In treating the chuckleheaded slave who feeds Jim, Tom acts as he did toward Jim earlier. The slave believes in witches, as did Jim. Consequently, Tom uses superstition to mystify him to the point of craziness, almost as he contrived with Jim. In fact, although, as Huck states, the Phelpses do not latch doors, Tom chooses to climb up the drainpipe to get into his bedroom, as Huck had to climb out of his room early in the book. As with leaving Jim money, so too, Tom, after further distressing the slave, gives him a ten cent piece. From Jim he and Huck get a hand squeeze of gratitude, Jim's human return for the whispered promise to set Jim free.

Much of what Tom foists on Huck and Jim as adventure is taken from the "best authorities," particularly historical romances such as Dumas's *The Man in the Iron Mask.* Pretensions are undercut by vulgar misunderstanding; we know that Tom's supposed knowledge is partly phony. Other chivalric sources of Tom's contrivances, carefully researched by Alan Gribben and Millicent Bell, include J. X. Boniface's *Picciola: The Prisoner of Fenestrella* (1836), Dumas's *The Count of Monte Cristo,* and the work which may have inspired his "Evasion," Dumas's *L'Evasion du Duc de Beaufort.*

Crucial to Tom's concept is "honor." As he announces at the beginning of chapter 35, there is more honor in getting Jim out through danger and difficulty; Tom's dreams reach to cutting Jim's leg off. In response to Huck's objection, however, he concedes that "Jim's a nigger and wouldn't understand the reasons for it, and how it's the custom in Europe." Like Colonel Sherburn's aside on the army, this almost unnoticeable comment brings in the concept of chivalry that was to receive more thorough treatment by Twain elsewhere. The leveling of Jim and Huck to pragmatists is thus begun, bound up in the racism of Tom's social position. Barnum, Twain, or any other advocate of education for blacks in the post–Civil War period would not have spoken as Tom speaks here. Tom is equally fraudulent in declaring this the most fun he has had and the "most intellectural." Honor, of course, is the driving force behind the Grangerford feud, the feud derived from a formalized code of behavior. Here honor may be a kind of individual self-centeredness. In both cases honor represents substitution of ideologies for personal feeling.

Tom's generalizations about Huck reach beyond simple argumentation and place Huck in the archetypal attitude of the American pioneer. As Tom says, "you don't ever seem to want to do anything that's regular, you want to be starting something fresh all the time." Huck, even in agreement with Tom, remains the pragmatist. Giving in to Tom's requirement of a rope ladder, he suggests a hickory bark ladder, which doesn't cost anything and won't make as much trouble for the boys as a stolen bed sheet. Furthermore, it is the material of the woods rather than an item of the material wealth of the farm. In true Twainian fashion, Tom builds on his destructiveness with the commandeered sheet by also demanding a shirt for the illiterate Jim to write on. Tom is still looking for the "troublesomest" way to proceed and still claiming that his mode alone is "regular," by which he means that it is according to the regulations which he himself creates. Tom, too, has his place as an American archetype representing the "go ahead" civilization-builders of the new nation.[24]

Tom's artificial romantic contrivances are a foil for Huck's subdued protests. They are introduced as the ultimate opposition to Huck's informed humanity; Tom's uninformed and self-oriented acts totally disregard the comfort, both physical and psychological, of others. This issue was evidenced as early as Twain's writings in the early sixties, in *Innocents Abroad* in the sabbath-day/horse riding incident in the Holy Land, and often made explicit in his shorter fiction. Consequently, the initial bamboozlement of Aunt Sally, by Tom-turned-Sid pretending to be a stranger and kissing her, is a notable offset to Huck's urgency to save the cruel betrayers, the Duke and the Dauphin. The theme of the last major portion of the novel is thus established as the interplay of actions and attitudes around regard towards others. Taken from this point of view, the last fifth of the book is far more compelling than critics describe it.

As the adventure to free Jim begins in earnest, a network of allusions contrasts kindness toward others with selfish principle. Tom, in effect, takes over the principled selfishness of Miss Watson's Providence and Pap's perverse "govment," even while all around him tendencies press in the opposite direction. On this plantation, all the people are kind. Huck's plan would make Jim just as free as Tom's. Huck's concern about Tom's seeming loss of pride causes him to be outraged on Tom's behalf (not his own). Tom is dissatisfied with an "easy and awkward" situation that allows success without honor—an attitude opposite to the pragmatic traditions of Americans from Ben Franklin and Thomas Jefferson down to the present. But it is at this very point in the narrative, chapter 35, that he names his list of sources—the "best authorities"—and wishes for the chance to saw off Jim's leg—an act far more dehumanizing than using the word "nigger," and to that extent a true test of the reader's perception of what is most important in human relations.

In chapter 35, Huck and Tom argue the point explicitly. Huck loses in the plot, but the reader's attitude is set. Tom is not merely a racist, he is a sexist and a class bigot as well, for he notes that only women and the common sort make ink out of rust and tears. He describes Jim as "captivated," another cacographic indication of his imperfect mastery of *The Iron Mask*, and continues recklessly by denying that anyone even needs to read Jim's writing once it is inscribed. Huck, while stealing tin plates, complains that "it's *somebody's* plates" that they are "wasting." Tom responds that the prisoner doesn't care and therefore it doesn't matter. The density of proofs that Tom is disregarding the Phelpses' welfare indicates the wider dimension of this novel's ending, in which Twain's view of society develops beyond the race issue.

A second discussion of borrowing and stealing, following the original discussion satisfactorily concluded by Huck and Jim on the raft, is carried on by Tom and Huck unsatisfactorily. We are again reminded that Pap (thus does Twain make sure that we reconnect Pap's influence with this portion of the narrative) called stealing "borrowing." Tom puts aside this assertion by saying that "representing" prisoners by stealing is not a crime, "it's his right." Tom thus uses to enthrall Huck the very phraseology of the people Huck was running from. The second half of this lengthy paragraph on stealing/borrowing contains Huck's anecdote about stealing a watermelon from the "nigger" patch; Tom makes him pay for it because he only wanted to eat it rather than to use it to smuggle a knife to kill a "seneskal." Huck, as with the doctrine of gifts in the opening, can't see "no advantage in representing a prisoner," and goes on to complain about having to "chaw over a lot of gold-leaf distinctions" just to "hog" a watermelon. Hogging a watermelon for Huck, like stealing Jim to freedom, is the level of reality he seeks—the level of reality common to Huck and Jim on the raft.

The chapter concludes with an expansion of Tom Sawyer's games. He reemphasizes the "right" way and the "regular" way as opposed to Huck's protest against "foolishness"; Tom's drive is toward being a "hero," as he says openly. *The Royal Path*, in its discussion of "Success," coolly notes youth is fascinated with brilliancy (239), but that maturity brings an appreciation for honest labor, elsewhere labeled the "littles" or details of life. Yet it is Huck who is turned down when he suggests using a pick-axe rather than case knives to free Jim; Tom wants to dig to China for thirty-seven years, to ape the books. Protesting that Jim doesn't know anybody in China, and to the time-scheme of thirty-seven years to free Jim, Huck complains, "he won't last." So much of Huck's protest parallels conventional protests against vanity, selfishness, and negative virtues in the battle of life that Tom is discredited almost line by line as his plans and design become ever more outrageous. Although the intensity of this criticism is cloaked in burlesque action, it provides an important symmetry in closing out the shore life as first seen in Huck's home town at the child level. The "play" of Tom's adventures, the enjoyment of pretended criminality, corresponds to the play of pride across a series of adventures involving the Grangerfords and Sherburn; the criticism of St. Petersburg is thus expanded even though the action takes place hundreds of miles down the river. Tom's "main point" is always the literary rather than the human objective. Huck's focus is always on Jim's real needs. The interplay is between fantasy and realism, with realist objectives clearly gaining our approval.

As Tom's evasion continues, his argument with Huck deepens, and his manipulation of Jim is developed beyond his manipulation of Aunt Polly in *Adventures of Tom Sawyer*. Each of the chapters from 36 through 40 elaborates Tom's treatment of Jim, expanding on the life of St. Petersburg or the raft. The following three chapters describe yet another stratum of local life and Jim and Huck's response to the wounded Tom. The novel is here seriocomic rather than melodramatic, in comparison to the shore scenes during the raft-voyage. The caricatures of romance, as developed in the authoritarian actions by Tom, draw the novel toward absurdity. The slapstick of the snakes escaping and the interplay of local farmers all lead away from Huck and Jim's quest for freedom. During the absurdity, Twain recasts his earlier themes in yet another guise that assures us that Huck and Jim are no better under Tom Sawyer's authority than they were under that of Miss Watson and Pap, establishing the poignancy of the novel's closing.

Freeing Jim, as a motive for Tom and Huck's actions, is at war with Tom's real motive: to generate adventures and glory. As this action progresses, it gives Huck numerous opportunities to make fun of "principles," as he does explicitly in chapter 36, and to attack adherence to rigid and distorted principles. Twain—and other literary comedians before him—consistently took this position. Tom is stuck with painful hands and an ethical problem: "It ain't right, and it ain't moral," but he concedes that he will use picks and "let on" it's case knives, even though he had earlier stated that right is right and wrong is wrong and anyone who is not ignorant and knows better should not do wrong. Tom even has to give up his lightning-rod entrances and come up the stairs, following Huck's advice to "let on it's a lightning rod." The travesty is highlighted against Huck's ethic: "Picks is the thing, moral or no moral. . . . When I start out to steal a nigger, or a watermelon, or a Sunday school book, I ain't no ways particular how it's done, so it's done. . . . I don't give a dead rat what the authorities thinks about it, nuther." Including Sunday school recalls earlier in the novel when Tom's fantasies were closely allied with it. Without clearly stating an irreligious viewpoint, Twain relates religious belief to impractical nonsense. Huck's attitude and the reader's preference for it, as developed by Twain, are set against intellectual and spiritual authorities as the easily corrupted resort of the self-aggrandizing, playing child. The last time a dead rat figured in the action, a covert alliance of religion and vulgarity, was during the funeral of Peter Wilks.

Jim's imprisonment confirms the nonsensicality of Tom's plots, now from the point of view of a partly willing victim. Consistent with Kenneth Burke's analysis of the repetition and development of themes toward a literary outcome, Twain has Jim approach Tom's authorities from the same position that Huck approached religious authorities, only more acceptingly, appropriate to his role as a black slave. Huck and Tom break into Jim's prison and find him looking, as Twain makes sure to note for the later contrast, hearty and healthy—the opposite of how the doctor who later saves Tom will find him after he has had to work for Tom's evasion: "I see plain enough he'd been worked main hard, lately." Instead of "clearing out without losing any time" as Jim wishes, however, Tom, disallowing the "unregular," insists on hearing Jim's story and making plans to send Jim unnecessary escape tools. Huck labels this "one of the most jackass ideas I ever struck," the first use of such a low level of language by any hero in a major novel in American literature. Likewise Jim "couldn't see no sense in the most of it, but he allowed we was white folks and knowed better than him." Twain aligns the issue of race with that of social belief and religious bigotry. Along with the "No,m', killed a nigger" remark, this comment firmly establishes the atmosphere of racism at the end of the novel. The pragmatic operator and the suffering slave thus allow the regular authoritarian, corrupting his sources to suit his game, to dictate the terms of their quest. Genteel Tom controls both, although one has damned himself to hell and the other is a chained prisoner. The power of humor to make such an awesomely discreditable venture into "boy" literature has been vastly underrated. Twain uses such humor to intellectualize events like witch burnings in *A Connecticut Yankee*; here, because the caricature interaction is more ludicrous, the awfulness seems the less. Yet Jim suffers. His suffering is muted in comic events rather than serious ones; for example he almost mashes out his teeth biting into a candlestick hidden in cornpone. The elaboration of comic action around the event further normalizes this new mode of life in which our urges for a successful outcome are baffled by the distortion of purpose in Tom. When to him it is the "best fun" and the "most intellectural," the misspelling of the last word is still another indicator of a malformed knowledge and purpose. The chapter is completed, appropriately, by abusing the mental stability of the slave Nat.

The comedy is oriented around the psychological discomfort—and real physical trouble—that Tom's activities create for others. The interplay between his doings and Huck and Jim's allegiance to practical kindness becomes a compelling motif hidden under the slapstick. Silas and Sally argue over Silas's missing shirt, stolen by Huck at Tom's direction. Slaves are yelled at for reporting stolen items. Uncle Silas is browbeaten; even spoon stealing gets to be part of the comic business driving Aunt Sally to distraction. As counterpoint, Huck and Tom fill rat holes for Uncle Silas out of guilt at the trouble they have caused. As he retreats confused from the already filled holes he has come to fill, Huck comments, "He was a nice old man. And always is." Niceness is the counterpoint to intellectual victimization. With Huck now subordinated, the tendencies that elevated the raft experience above common society are reversed. Tom captures the irony of his own "vicarious sacrifice" much like the Artemus Ward who offered up his uncles and cousins to fight the Civil War—Tom sets Jim to carving inscriptions on a grindstone and when Jim complains, Huck reports that "Tom said he would let me help him do it." Tom's treatment of physical things shows his excesses, his wasteful disregard of food and goods. Aping the romances of imprisonment, Tom and Huck smuggle tooth-breaking junk in a pie; later, eating a sawdust pie almost poisons them. The sheet rope they were going to use is mostly thrown away—more waste of Aunt Sally's things. They steal a warming pan beloved by Uncle Silas, "because it belonged to one of his ancestors with a long wooden handle that come over from England with William the Conqueror in the Mayflower or one of them early ships." Perhaps most excessive is enrolling Jim in the nobility with a coat of arms and into the workforce with slave labor.

Twain's coat of arms for Jim is one of his funniest uses of the simple ironic caricature. Jim as a "state" prisoner has to have a coat of arms. Tom's chivalric invention features a dog couchant with a chain "embattled" under his foot representing slavery: "crest, a runaway nigger, *sable,* with his bundle over his shoulder on a bar sinister; and a couple of gules for supporters, which is you and me." The emblem of the fugitive slave posters, the silhouette of the runaway with his bundle, is here integrated into the heraldic language, making the two societies allies by mingling their symbols. Rolling a grindstone back to Jim's cell, Huck and Tom find it too heavy for them and Tom creates in life the picture he created as a crest: "We see it warn't no use, so we got to go and fetch Jim. So he raised up his bed and slid the chain off of the bed-leg, and wrapt it round and round his neck, and we crawled out through our hole and down there, and Jim and me laid into that grindstone and walked her along like nothing; and Tom superintended. He could out-superintend any boy I ever see. He knowed how to do everything." The obvious ironies of the evasion identify Tom not only as a creator of others' hardships, but as a cynic who allows others to carry out the sacrifices he invents for them. Jim is depicted with chain; Huck and Tom are the "gules" or fools accompanying him, an obvious pun on the Elizabethan idea of "gulls" being foolish people and the heraldry color red. The intellectual artifact reenacted as comedy is Tom's alternative to the raft life.

The raft life is itself echoed, evidence of the small heroisms of Jim and Huck, at variance with Tom's quest for glory. Two of the four comic phrases Tom gives Jim to inscribe carry echoes of the Duke and the Dauphin. The fourth refers to the natural son of Louis XIV, recalling the Dauphin's pretensions to be a son of the house of Louis. The first, and possibly the third, recapture the language of the two frauds as they invaded the raft, and their fake authoritarian supremacy as developed earlier is filtered into Tom's activities. Tom introduces snakes and bugs into Jim's previously comfortable hut. He proposes rattlesnakes, but Jim says he would run through the wall; we remember that Huck had played tricks on Jim using snakes which almost killed him. Tom argues that since every animal is grateful for kindness, Jim must pet the snakes. Jim refuses to wrap them—like the chain he carried to roll the grindstone—around his neck and begins complaining about the hardship of being a prisoner. Tom suggests playing painful music, including the religious song "The Last Link is Broken," and says that the rats and snakes and spiders will just swarm over Jim and have a "noble" good time. Jim responds with a statement derived from the raft: "Yes, *dey* will, I reck'n, mars Tom, but what kine er time is *Jim* havin'? Blest if I kin see de pint. But I'll do it, ef I got to. I reck'n I better keep de animals satisfied, en not have no trouble in de house." What you want on a raft, in Huck and Jim's parlance, is for everyone to feel right and kind towards the others. Now, converted to this burlesque situation, Huck and Jim's discovery, their rule of conduct, becomes the rule of conduct even in the face of frustrating nonsense. In caricature, elements of religion and social prestige belong to Tom, the creator of meaningless silliness; putting up with the nonsense and getting by belongs to the common men—Jim and Huck, pragmatists. The trouble and worry of raising flowers with tears is similar; Jim complains that they'll die on his hands because he scarcely ever cries.

The interplay between kindness and callousness continues. Snakes for Jim's hut escape in Aunt Sally's house, and Huck provides a long comic passage on the snakes dripping from rafters and Aunt Sally's emotional distress. The passage ends in dead-pan humor on women's psychology which escapes into callousness, possibly the only such point in the book, references to Jim included. Jim is made uncomfortable by Tom's imported vermin, and the boys get terrible bellyaches from eating sawdust to conceal their activities. Every figure in the book is subjected to significant discomfort by Tom's imagination. This is counterpart to the induction into the raft adventure, when Jim and Huck retreat under Jim's advice and with Huck's provisions to the cave on Jackson's Island, vastly improving their immediate physical comfort. *The Royal Path* flatly condemns courage that is overdone as "rashness." Useless and impossible efforts waste vigor and spirit and should be restrained and well directed (218). Tom is not restrained and his bragging and seeking after the "gaudy" not only create the distresses already noticed, but continue to jeopardize Tom himself. Tom's rashness will ultimately be demonstrated when his contrivances result in his own, near-fatal wounding.

The actual "evasion," "three weeks" after Tom's early activities, begins with Tom's disgust at the "confiding and mullet-headed" Aunt Sally and Uncle Silas. In his reversal of the ideals of conduct, Tom continues to demand that Huck and he carry out the romantic devices as their *duty*, "and not worry about whether anybody *sees* us do it or not."

He concludes by asking Huck if he hasn't got "no principle at all?" The heavy use of the words "principle" and "duty" are an obvious travesty of children's literature. The open skepticism towards principles places the book directly in the stream of literary comedy of the post–Civil War period.

The "grand bulge" is begun with a lengthy burlesque letter using the same fraudulent poses employed by the Dauphin to fleece the camp meeting. The letter pretends to tip the hand of a gang planning to kidnap the slave to the Ingean Territory (Twain referring to the locus of a possible sequel following this novel, already anticipating future adventures). Talk of doing the right thing and getting "religgion" undercut the note's rhetoric, making it not only boy-fun but also subliterate. As in many areas of this and other of Twain's novels, the humor is intellectualized, rather than restrained by strict realism. The image projected of Tom in action is a game for the reader to play out with the author more so than in other realist novels. Travesty appears in the idea that the thief who should blow a tin horn will really *baa* like a sheep to help the farmers. Certainly Twain had in mind boybooks; he goes beyond them in burlesquing his own character, Tom, through his inappropriate devices. The intellectualization is far different from the intellectualization in a Henry James novel, but it is nonetheless effective.

Below the level of social wrong to Jim is the level of denial of Huck's pragmatism, the substitution of manipulated fear for kindness, the substitution of verminous discomfort for the easy and comfortable, and the transformation of real actions into grotesque distortions of book actions. With so many layers of significance, the novel is as dense at this point as at any time during the river journey, even while a sophisticated reader will find it most dissatisfying in the subordination of the hero to the false leadership of the restrictive authorities who the hero had earlier fled. Indeed, it is hard to remember that Huck's flight was never fully successful; all too soon the raft became dominated by the Duke and Dauphin. At this point in the novel, readers grant Huck and Jim a far greater degree of success—thanks to Twain's imagery and elaboration of moments—than Twain ever granted them in the actual plot. As a puzzle, these points merit further consideration in treating how the reader comes to a sense of success at the end of the book.

Beginning the final adventure, Tom sends Huck back to Aunt Sally's cellar for butter, allowing Huck to discover fifteen armed farmers.

This should not be surprising to the reader who recalls that Uncle Silas's town tarred and feathered the Duke and Dauphin, foreshadowing the active violence of present events. Huck, hiding the butter on his head, tells us he didn't take his hat off, all the same—thus comically alluding to the involutions of Tom's plan in establishing the basis for Aunt Sally's manic concern. She will think that the melting butter is Huck's brains oozing out. Twain takes this opportunity to dramatize the true affection which is being transgressed by the evasion; Huck will later see her old gray head nodding at the window, as Twain blatantly develops this theme to the point of bathos. Typical of other parts of this sequence, Twain includes a comic line when Aunt Sally exclaims that the butter was just the color of Huck's brains. Such lines are part of the continuing reinforcement of the reader's perception that this is a comic novel. The reader intellectualizes events as "humor." Huck, now at his most pragmatic, wants nothing more than to "tell Tom how we'd overdone this thing" so that they could "stop fooling around." Tom responds with the opposite of Huck's pragmatism: "His eyes just blazed" at the very moment that armed men tramp through the dark with intentions of killing the culprits. We know that Tom's excitement is based on contrivance, not reality, even if we participate in it superficially—Twain's comic device is not at all simple. The chase scene which follows includes a break for the river with dogs, suggesting the Grangerford episode.

It is easy to lose the importance of Huck's manner of narration in the rush of events. Huck's deadpan represents controlled doubts, mingled with the insight of trained experience. He notes that the boys can hear the men "because they wore boots, and yelled, but we didn't wear no boots, and didn't yell." First-person dead-pan narration is so close to an omniscient overview that we can understand how the intellectualization of humor blends into the seemingly spoken narrative of Huck. Noting how many times Huck comments similarly, we can understand why it is that he seems so like Twain's Hank Morgan and Pudd'nhead Wilson, both highly proficient adults. Only viscerally, not intellectually, do we recall his competence in staging his own murder, many chapters before.

The climax of the "evasion" is relatively brief. Huck, Jim, and Tom flee in the dark, are shot at, and arrive at Huck's raft with a series of escalating congratulations that is typical of Twain's use of the ironic anticlimax. First, Huck congratulates Jim on being free again, never to be a slave no more. Immediately, Jim congratulates Huck on Tom's behalf that it was "planned" and "done" beautiful—"mixed up en splendid," being the further correctly ironic restatement of the muddleheadedness of Tom's design. Third, and finally, Tom "was the gladdest of all because he had a bullet in the calf of his leg." The verbal takeoff point is Huck and Jim's great ambition. Tom's fantasy provides the second level of comic response to Huck and Jim's real issue. Tom's reality, fulfilling the most self-destructive aspect of his romancing, is the culminating discomfort, short of death. The boys have arrived at the final outcome of Tom's vision, but its consequences will be the recapture of Jim. Jim and Huck refuse to continue unless Tom is treated by a doctor. Yet another irony is offered as Huck acknowledges that he knew Jim was "white inside," in his loyalty.

The escape, shooting, and saving of Tom is similar to a whole subgenre of American literature that stands outside the traditional romances Twain burlesques through Tom Sawyer's evasion. The prison escape literature of the Civil War provides much of the sort of episodic suspense and development captured here. One such source is by M. Quod (Charles Bertrand Lewis, 1842–1924), a well-known humorist of the period who specialized in the 1880s in black dialect humor, publishing a collection under the title *Brother Gardner's Lime-Kiln Club* in 1882. His "Beyond the Picket Lines; or, the Army Reminiscences of Captain Jack" appeared in *Ballou's Monthly Magazine* (39:260–271) of March 1874. Civil War escape literature carries its own excitement, but M. Quod's piece, while not necessarily a direct source for *Huck Finn,* has so many similarities that a comparison will indicate where authors found sources of excitement and tension to enhance their action. A scout, a Union captain, is sent to spy on Fredericksburg by Union generals. He first attempts to cross the river outside the city on a small makeshift raft; as the raft sinks, he leaps into a rowboat being rowed by an oblivious escaping slave named Jim. After he joins forces with Jim, they hide together and eventually enter Fredericksburg, several times being caught or almost caught and escaping through disguise and flight. Jim and the captain finally escape in a rowboat after the last adventure, but the scout is almost killed when soldiers firing on them graze his head with a shot. Thus, Tom Sawyer's fate is suggested. But the story also projects some of the atmosphere of Huck and Jim as well. In several instances the two rejoin through impossible coincidence, much like Huck and Jim coming together after the storm. The story concludes as the narrator tells us that the attack on Fredericks-

burg continued because the northern press and public clamored for
battle, despite reports of troops waiting for the Union charge. In other
words, publicity—Tom Sawyer's goal—spurred a poor military decision. The excitement of adventure and escape is a sure-fire element in
each story; the futility of the outcome is another. In addition, however,
comes the close partnership of white and black, with the slave's wisdom as important to success as the white's. The captain's wound is an
outcome of commitment to cause, but comes almost as an after-
thought in the last lines of a long story. For Tom, however, the wound
serves an ironic purpose. In case the Jim in Huck's story may seem too
accepting of Tom's control to modern readers, the escaping Jim in M.
Quod's story is equally ready to join his interests with his new friend—
and this readiness to join almost without question, and with respect,
is a common element in both stories. A similar uniting of forces in
Cudjo's Cave by Trowbridge is, alternatively, carefully analyzed and
explained by the dubious black hero who engineers it. The unity of
purpose to aid the Union army, the unity of races—white soldier and
black slave—the excitement of escape and disguise played out within
America's climactic historic moment, all provide us with a context for
the components of Twain's ending which suggests a special American-
ness. Since the story appeared in 1874, it is intriguing to think that it,
along with *Cudjo's Cave*, influenced Twain. Even if the story itself did
not, however, the naturalness of the slave-white events is established
by their commonality. These are the materials common in the American epic; *Huck Finn* as one of the few leading contenders to be the
great American epic rightfully draws on such sources.

— 11 —

Tying Up the Loose Ends

The final three chapters of *Adventures of Huckleberry Finn* conclude the novel appropriately to Twain's sense of the real world. He makes sure that we do not conclude that Huck's vulgarity is the source of his humanity by showing us unattractive vernacular speakers. He reduces Tom below the level of common decency by allowing Jim to suffer while Tom recovers consciousness from his self-developed, if not self-inflicted, wound. And he allows Huck the only assertion of power that is available to heroes like Huck, Hank, Pudd'nhead, and Tom Canty— rejection of the society around them, for Huck by a declaration of flight.

The yokels are significant in the completion of the novel. Scholars have contended that Huck's vulgar vernacular language holds some key to his insight, although earlier comic figures such as Sut Lovingood show none of Huck's sympathy for others. Twain's yokels disabuse us of any endorsement of the vulgar. During an extended discussion of Tom's devices, a series of speakers demonstrate the yokel perspective, and none of the portraits is flattering. More than a mere exercise in vernacular comedy, the episode sets the farmers apart from the readers. The first and "worst" is Old Mrs. Hotchkiss; with a maddeningly declamatory and repetitive style, she concludes that the "nigger's" crazy as "Nebokoodneezer." However justified by the evidence, she is clearly a fool. Mrs. Damrell, sister Utterback—a name used in one of Twain's earliest published pieces for another vulgar country-woman—Brer Penrod and Brer Hightower follow in succession. As the countryfolk wolf down breakfast slathered in molasses, their astonishment at Tom's doings is punctuated with trite speech ("dog my cats"), vulgarisms ("s'I" for "I said"), and so on. One of the yokel women even proposes that there must have been a "raft uv 'm" at work, and concludes that she'd give two dollars to have the supposedly secret African writing on Silas's shirt read to her, and then lash the "niggers" that wrote it. Venal money-centeredness, savagery toward the Negro, and ignorance are woven together in the coarse scene. Its humor lacks overt violence, and after the melodrama of the rest of the novel, it seems a quiet time of little consequence in the plot even though its meaning is important.

Aunt Sally is part of the yokel chorus, enumerating things taken by Huck and Tom, but she is also separate from and somewhat above it. Her speech seems more ignorant in this passage than elsewhere, pocked with phrases like "hide nor hair," "they slides," "under our noses." Socially insensitive to slaves, she is ignorant and superstitious, presuming that "*sperits* couldn't a done better." But, she subjects Huck to mothering so good as to make him feel mean; Huck responds directly to her kindness, and her appeal to Huck to "be good for my sake" freezes him; he sneaks out only to see her sitting by a candle in the window in a pathetic picture of the loyal mother. She is a final womanly image of kindness, a picture of pathos bordering on bathos.

The doctor who heals Tom has the kindly traits common to other Twainian professionals, and his attitude corresponds to Huck's knowledge. Huck recruits the doctor by telling him of the "singular dream" which shot Tom. The doctor, as pragmatic as Huck, scarcely comments on this oddity except to make more explicit the irony already implicit in Tom's exploit. When the doctor reappears with Tom Sawyer, Jim is brought along behind as he was found, in a calico dress. When Jim is mistreated, the doctor intervenes mildly, saying that Jim "ain't a bad nigger," a dubious compliment. When the doctor needed help to aid Tom, Jim came to the rescue even though he had to give up hiding. The doctor, in the retelling, is so focussed on his own needs that the reader feels the irony of Jim's unrecognized sacrifice. The doctor comments that Jim's aid, particularly since Jim appeared to have been overworked by some recent owner, made him "worth a thousand dollars—and kind treatment, too." Valuing people in money terms represents the failure of this society.

The farmers demonstrate their meanness by cuffing Jim. The only restraint on their hanging Jim as an example is that since he "ain't our nigger" they would have to pay for him. Huck moralizes that those who most want their "satisfaction" out of a hanging of a "nigger" are not the ones most ready to pay for him. The men's violence is directed at the slave who had not done "just right" and made a "raft" of trouble; the main themes of the novel continue as faint echoes in the word choice. Like Pap, the farmers conclude by tapering off with a "generl goodbye cussing." In response to the doctor's plea for Jim, they stop cussing him, but they do not remove his "rotten heavy" chains. Cupidity, ignorance, cussing, and self-centeredness mark the local figures, ameliorated only by the doctor. These men are no backwoods heroes, romanticized by Twain into paragons of intuitive humanity outside social boundaries.

The word "kind" is only a faint echo of the raft concept, but a meaningful one. The ethic of Tom's world is reestablished as dominant; no longer do the feelings of the raft control the action, if they ever really had.

The doctor repeats the idea, after describing Jim's tenderness toward Tom and his docility, that Jim "ain't no bad nigger." Huck completes the irony of this racism by being thankful to the doctor for "doing Jim that good turn." To insure that the irony is sufficiently thick even for an obtuse reader, Twain has Huck reemphasize that the doctor was a man with a "good" heart. Jim is rewarded, appropriately to the irony, for every farmer "promised right out and hearty, that they wouldn't cuss him no more." But his chains are not removed, and meat and greens are not added to Jim's bread and water, Huck laments. Huck is reduced to virtual helplessness, planning to work on Aunt Sally to improve Jim's lot. The reader's sensitivity to Jim is larger than the characters', guaranteeing that our sense of an inhuman society is reinforced. Twain's writings always reflect an appreciation of the trained professional, but here, even he shows a blindness toward humanity. How could it be elsewise, since even Huck, sensitized as he is to Jim as his friend, cleaves to the same social perspectives. Huck's determination to improve Jim's lot is covert; he dares make no active protest, a reminder that this is not a novel of social change, but of individual allegiance and personal values.

When Tom regains consciousness, the adventure is hot on his lips; he begins to retell it immediately, braggart that he is, declaring it was "bully." The mental distress to Aunt Sally is transformed into comic interaction between her and Tom until Jim is brought up and revealed to be "safe and sound," on bread and water, loaded down with chains. Tom responds with moral outrage in a picture that carries its irony to an alert reader: "his nostrils opening and shutting like gills," he declares that they have no "right" to shut Jim up, for "he's as free as any cretur that walks this earth!" Talk of rights has been suspicious since Pap and the *Walter Scott* robbers indulged in it. Tom's noble statement is universalized by its reference to earth and its creatures, almost like biblical laws, but it rings hollow because of the narrative recount just given. Tom's contrived events were qualitatively different from those recounted by Huck so convincingly in chapter 31. The repeated forms of events propel us to further senses of a gulf of applied humanity between Tom, who speaks high-sounding phrases, and Huck, who lives in often powerless invisibility. Twain demonstrates not only differences in social perspective but also differences personally between the private conscience and the public seeker of vain-glory. Yet, most first-time readers are likely to thrill to Tom's statement as an ultimate freeing of Jim; they will be far less sensitive to the irony of the statement in context than an analytic reader reviewing the action. Twain thus achieves a double effect, which is partly in conflict with itself, as I believe he intended.

In terms compatible with the philosophy of Kenneth Burke, the novel has succeeded better than detractors of the "last fifth" envision. Crucial words like "rights," "raft," "sivilization," and "kind" recur both as informational words and as words in different contexts, as when "raft" is used in "a whole raft of troubles" or elevated by hyphenation to "raft-voyage." Twain as a master of symbolic language has provided powerful echoes of his major themes underlying the melodrama of the plot. His many episodes allow him to play and replay relationships in different guises. The symphonic repetition of Huck's relationships with women is notable, first as an apprentice with Mrs. Loftus, later as the catspaw of Sophia Grangerford, still later as the helper and prayed-for stranger-friend of Mary Jane Wilks, and finally as the covertly sympathetic viewer of Aunt Sally. In each case, the tension, expectation, frustration, and catharsis of the contained episode add to the tension which crescendoed in Mary Jane's determination to pray for Huck as Judas. The expanded power of such moments is true evidence of Twain as a literary artist.

Tying Up the Loose Ends

As the Great American Novel *Adventures of Huckleberry Finn* would have to show evidence of the highest level of art as vision. The Concord Public Library's objection to the novel, along with critics such as Robert Bridges, was based on its realism—a realism repulsive to some Victorians by being developed in comic and intellectual terms through the managed vulgar voice of Huck speaking for Mark Twain. To them, Huck was a bad example because he was vulgar, and because he was tarred by the depicted violence and criminality surrounding him. The realist element in the book was its source of trouble, not Huck's position as a social outsider and dissident. That position has precedents in moral philosophy as reflected in *The Royal Path of Life* and in fiction as reflected in J. T. Trowbridge's stories. Concord's dislike of the book derived from its success in clothing Twain's attack on inhumanity in a veneer of reality.

The resolution of moral issues rises to a universal level. The joint climax of Huck's decision to free Jim and Mary Jane's endorsement of Huck gives the book a deceptive ending before the ending. The moral issues of Huck and Jim are resolved, but Huck's adventures, as such, are by no means at an end. The greatest adventure of all is his return to Tom's domination, for that return tests and develops the independence not of Huck but of the reader. Twain never contended that man was perfectible. In fact, in *A Connecticut Yankee* four years later, Yankee Hank's "man factories" are notably unsuccessful when challenged by superstition and early training. Critics who wish *Huck Finn* to end differently than it does are wishing that it become a book inconsistent with Twain's philosophy generally. Huck does indeed leap to visionary greatness, but his society does not change, nor does his background, training, or set of beliefs. His determination to "go to hell" is an obvious key. The Concordians resented the degraded surroundings and language, so seldom seen in orthodox child literature, and the scepticism toward religion, which is consistent with Twain's general doubts about the betterment of man as a race. Ultimately, they may not have been rejecting the rebel from society and his own fate.

The last fifth of the novel finishes the business of discrediting authority. Tom's travesties of romance undercut the world which Huck and Jim attempted to leave. General readers find this portion of the book funny and fast-paced; they are opposed by professional authors and critics, who find it a let-down. However, its business is still serious. Huck and the vernacular farmers do not control destiny. Huck's helplessness in the face of Tom is no different from his helplessness in the face of the Duke and Dauphin; it is played out in a more elaborate burlesque of juvenile behavior, but it is just as perilous and freedom-denying to Jim. Both episodes are based on the false premise of Jim as an escaped and recaptured slave. Grant that the absurdity of human slavery is allowable, and all other absurdities become merely window dressing—as Twain joked about the death penalty and financial compensation in Chinese "taels" for the Boxer Rebellion years later, "Taels I win, Heads you lose."[25] Twain's belief in individual kindness causes Huck to leap out of the social mire only in his last lines. In that leap, Huck reconfirms his standing as an individual. And in that standing as an individual he reconfirms our sense that a democratic man, an individual, is the greatest outcome of our corporate society, and is higher than the various social and religious authorities that pervert his conscience. As Twain is an egalitarian philosopher, his philosophy is rooted in this optimism, so at variance with the universal pessimism he held about the intrinsic nature of man.

Adventures of Huckleberry Finn is a fusion of Twain's experience, itself quintessentially representative of nineteenth-century America. Huck's psychology reflects Twain's own psychology almost certainly, his need for acceptance and his yearning for social success. At the same time, it embodies American ideals in its views of the relation between society, politics, and the individual. Victorian sources like *The Royal Path*, Stowe's and Beecher's writings, and J. T. Trowbridge's fiction all demonstrate Twain's relatedness to the fund of moral philosophy, social belief, and dramatic imagery of his times. The novel is both a summary and an elevation of the highest hopes of American ethical idealism in its period. That Twain found a compelling natural imagery in the Mississippi River and the shore-life surrounding it completes the range of American components of this vision, fusing the regional, national, and universal in Huck's journey.

Tom's portion of the explanation in the last chapter is that Miss Watson set Jim free in her will. She felt shame, taking over Huck's burden of shame, that she would sell him down the river—a good response, though not a full renunciation of slavery. Tom explains his own motivation as *"adventure,"* a willingness, swashbuckling in the extreme, to "wade neck-deep in blood." A burlesque statement rather than a sensible one, it nonetheless implies a kinship with the Granger-fords and Colonel Sherburn natural to Tom. Huck now understands how Tom, with "his bringing up," could have conspired "to set a free nigger free." The social background of St. Petersburg is maintained to the very end unchanged and unenlightened, and Tom's place in it likewise. Even religion comes in for a last gratuitous insult as Huck notes that the revelations of altered identities and events make Silas so drunk that his next prayer-meeting sermon gave him "a rattling reputation, because the oldest man in the world couldn't a understood it." Thus, the debunking of religion in relation to Tom's activities both at the start and the end of the book forms a continuity. The revelation that Tom had stolen and hidden letters from Aunt Polly is a last lowering of his activities back to boyhood impudence.

"Chapter the Last" provides a proper conclusion appropriate to the Victorian novel. Tom's plan to continue the adventures down the Mississippi—continuing Jim's anxiety—is explained to Huck with the payoff being a payoff: Tom planned to set things to rights by paying Jim for his lost time—not his wasted feeling. Then, Tom, true to his egocentric "style," would ride Jim home on a steamboat "in style" to be greeted by the other "niggers." Tom pleases Jim most to death by giving him forty dollars for his troubles—the identical amount of "dirty" dollars that the Dauphin sold him out for. Equally significant, the kind Aunt Sally and Uncle Silas make a "heap of fuss" over Jim for his loyalty to Tom and "give him all he wanted to eat, and a good time, and nothing to do," rewards more consistent with the physical immediacy that provided a key ingredient of the raft-voyage. Jim's hairy-breast boast recalls Jackson's Island; the idea of riches carries with it our recollection that Jim hopes one day to buy freedom for his wife and children.

Sentence by sentence the novel rolls towards it conclusion. Twain establishes a third reference to the Injun Territory to provide a basis for the sequel. Jim joins in the revelation of suppressed knowledge by revealing his knowledge that Pap Finn was dead—thus reenacting, at his level, what Tom did to him. The reduplicating act of withholding freeing knowledge indicts Jim as part of the overreaching web of society in which Huck, and Tom, and the rest all join; it is a significantly unifying revelation and important in completing the basis for Huck's final statement. Also, it is necessary to bring back into the text a last echoing note of Pap as a corrupter of political life and social causes.

The concluding paragraph describes the outcomes as logical ones. Tom's vanity is represented by the watch-chain. Huck's promise that he won't try and make any more books because it is "rotten" trouble has resonances with the larger plot which he has lived as well as written, even though a sense of authorial intrusion per se has not been stressed. The projection of the sequel into the "Territory" leaves room for Twain to write a follow-up narrative, of course, but it also does more. The Territory is yet a wilder and freer place than the river, and it promises a recapturing of the emotional and ethical highpoints of the novel. The Territory offers an optimistic rather than a pessimistic horizon. Huck's reasons expand that sense to a visionary one, yet another statement implying a reprise of all the previous action—"aunt Sally she's going to adopt me and sivilize me and I can't stand it. I been there before." And now, truly, Huck rises to greatness again, after his subordination to Tom Sawyer, for this line recaptures all the suggestions of the earlier uses of the word "sivilization" during the reign of Miss Watson and Pap: cramping, restricting, isolating, and dehumanizing Huck. At the same time, in its breadth it suggests the entire raft-voyage with the encounters on shore that set Huck and Jim and the raft apart from the world of affairs. And finally, it implies a growth beyond the world dominated by Tom Sawyer, who is preeminently "sivilization's" leading exponent, and its most dominant one at both ends of the adventure. Even if Huck has not outgrown Tom, in the American frontier lies Huck's future for us as readers.

The sign-off, "The End, Yours truly, Huck Finn," is similar to the ending Artemus Ward applied to his comic works in the 1860s and unabashedly places the book in the tradition of the literary comedians, those boasters of egalitarian skepticism towards all things official. Huck has not been an intrusive narrator, especially because at times he was either close to omniscient—or close to Mark Twain the comedian. I have elsewhere argued the case for Twain's debt to Ward, but the placement of the last page within a tradition—within a genre, and that not a particularly elevated genre as the Victorian world saw literature—continues to be significant. The literary comedians during the Civil War were the Union's staunch defenders. The issue of slavery blended for them with the issue of humanity, even in some cases such as Ward's where the original viewpoint on abolition was lukewarm— like Twain's own. In opposition to established social dicta, they boasted a more common route to the values of humanity, the recognition of human nature as a touchstone for moral responsibility, and the acceptance of the lowness of humanity. They opposed the posturing self-indulgent romanticism of the preceding era which Twain made his foil through Tom Sawyer. The values are brought home by the simply but correctly spelled salutation, following the one perverse "s" of the outer world's intent. The narrower world is ultimately to be

defeated by Huck's determination that if he couldn't stand "sivilization" as it was, he could go outside it once again as a fully realized
mythic American spirit and try it as it wasn't. The final words in the
book are appropriately his own name, and not now lies, but truth:
"THE END, YOURS TRULY, HUCK FINN"

Notes

1. William Gilmore Simms, "The Philosophy of the Omnibus," *Godey's* 23 (September 1841):107.

2. Rollin Osterweis, *The Myth of the Lost Cause, 1865–1900* (Hamden, Conn.: Archon Books, 1973). Nor did the question go away; literary comedian Marietta Holley still fulminated over it in 1892 in *Samantha on the Race Problem.*

3. I am indebted to Professor Fishkin for information about the resurgence of racism as evidenced in newspapers. See the entry "Civil Rights Bill" in *A Dictionary of American Politics* (New York: A. L. Burt, 1888), 94–95, for a reflection of these events by a contemporaneous narrator.

4. The *New York Times* of 14 March 1985 carried a front-page article by Edwin McDowell entitled "From Twain, a Letter on Debt to Blacks," which described a newly discovered letter by Twain identifying Warren T. McGuin as the black student whose tuition he paid for study at the Yale University Law School.

5. Clara Clemens, *My Father Mark Twain* (New York: Harper & Brothers, 1931), 51.

6. As quoted in the *Boston Transcript* for 17 March 1885. The *Springfield Republican* went on to assign Twain's works to the moral level of the dime novels, seeing *Huck Finn* as degenerating into "gross trifling with every fine feeling," as the author had at the Whittier Dinner; western Massachusetts was not ready to forgive skepticism in the land of Longfellow, even if Oliver Wendell Holmes and other sophisticated literati could take Twain on his own terms.

7. Louis Budd, *Our Mark Twain: The Making of His Public Personality* (Philadelphia: University of Pennsylvania Press, 1983).

8. Edgar Lee Masters, *Mark Twain: A Portrait* (New York: Charles Scribner's Sons, 1938), 134.

9. Alan Gribben, "'I Did Wish Tom Sawyer Was There': Boy-Book Elements in *Tom Sawyer* and *Huckleberry Finn*," in *One Hundred Years of*

Huckleberry Finn, edited by Robert Sattelmeyer and J. Donald Crowley (Columbia: University of Missouri Press, 1985), 149–70.

10. Among similar works one prominent title is Mrs. Helen Campbell's *Darkness and Daylight, or Lights and Shadows of New York Life* (Hartford: A. D. Worthington & Co., 1892).

11. Richard Dorsan, *Jonathan Draws the Longbow* (Cambridge: Harvard University Press, 1946), 70–71.

12. Richard Rubinstein, in *The Cunning of History* (New York: Harper, 1975), has recently used the same point to identify the elimination of races in terms of "surplus people" along the same lines; in the widespread tacit acceptance of the Holocaust, surplus Jews were left to destruction during the war years, while useful Nazi corporate managers and military personnel were quickly reintegrated into the victors' military establishments thereafter.

13. See David E. E. Sloane, *Mark Twain as a Literary Comedian* (Baton Rouge: Louisiana State University Press, 1979) for an extended discussion of this point. See also Leah A. Strong, *Joseph Hopkins Twichell* (Athens: University of Georgia Press, 1966), 109–50.

14. Identified by Caroline Ticknor in 1916 and readily available in the 1944 Heritage Press edition's appendix (412–16).

15. One such study featured an outraged Yankee rube who would have demanded his money back from the fraudulent show, but couldn't because he sneaked in. The story is reprinted from *Yankee Notions* in David E. E. Sloane, *The Literary Humor of the Urban Northeast, 1830–1890* (Baton Rouge: Louisiana State University Press, 1983).

16. Huck's dialect allows him to be even more forceful than more elevated characters in Howells's *The Rise of Silas Lapham*, who caricatured the sentimental "Tears, Idle Tears" as "Slop, Silly Slop" but went no further.

17. See Victor Fischer's note to the text, page 416, in the California edition.

18. See the 1869 edition as reprinted by the Stowe-Day Foundation of Hartford, Connecticut (1985), 205–6.

19. Similarly, a pro-slavery farmer in *Cudjo's Cave* identified having "big knowin' niggers" around as "too much like sleeping on a row of powder barrels, with lighted candles stuck in the bungholes" (224). It is possible that the metaphor creeps into *Huck Finn* at this point in the action because of the influence of the earlier work on Twain's imagination.

20. See Franklin Rogers, *Mark Twain's Burlesque Patterns as Seen in the Novels and Narratives, 1855–1885* (Dallas: Southern Methodist University Press, 1960).

21. Published in 1876 by W. C. King and Co. of Springfield, Massachusetts, and by the Western Publishing House of Chicago; the 1881 edition is cited here.

Notes

22. See Alice Fisher's *The Drama of the Gifted Child*, R. D. Laing's *The Politics of Experience*, and Sigmund Freud's *Civilization and Its Discontents* for elaboration of these psychological issues.

23. *What Is Man? and Other Essays* (New York: Harper & Bros., 1917), 17.

24. See Daniel Boorstin, *The Americans/The Colonial Experience* (New York: Random House, 1958), for an expansion of this characteristic.

25. In "To the Person Sitting in Darkness."

Bibliography

Primary Sources

Editions of Adventures of Huckleberry Finn

The first English edition was published by Chatto & Windus, London, in 1884; the first U.S. edition was published by Charles L. Webster & Co., New York, 1885.

Blair, Walter, and Fischer, Victor, editors. Berkeley: University of California Press, 1985. This is intended to be the definitive edition, using the original illustrations and format but reinserting the flatboatmen passage and correcting the text to Twain's "intention" rather than to the first edition as such; extensive notes document real people and places adapted into the novel as well as matters of language and text.

Bradley, Sculley, et al., editors. New York: W. W. Norton, 1961. Norton Critical Edition including valuable contemporary sources, among which is Hooper's "Simon Suggs Attends a Camp Meeting," and extensive excerpts from major critics. The flatboatmen passage is included among other source materials.

Budd, Louis J., editor. Adventures of Huckleberry Finn (A Facsimile of the Manuscript). 2 vols. Detroit: Gale Research Company, 1983. With introduction and afterword.

Hill, Hamlin, editor. New York: Harper & Row Publishers, 1987. Facsimile of the first American edition of 1885 with an excellent introduction and bibliography by the editor, updated from the 1962 edition of the same text.

Smith, Henry Nash, editor. Boston: Houghton Mifflin Company, 1958. Introduction and commentary on the text by the editor, acknowledged dean of Mark Twain critics up to the time of his death.

Bibliography

Other Works

The Adventures of Tom Sawyer. Hartford: American Publishing Co., 1876.

The Autobiography of Mark Twain. Edited by Charles Neider. New York: Washington Square Press, 1961.

Life on the Mississippi. New York: Heritage Press, 1944 (1883).

What Is Man? and Other Essays. New York: Harper & Bros., 1917 (1906).

The Writings of Mark Twain. "Author's National Edition," 24 vols. New York: Harper & Brothers, n.d.

Secondary Sources

Huckleberry Finn has been the subject of important critical documents by Lionel Trilling, Van Wyck Brooks, Bernard DeVoto and others that have significance in their own right. These will be found in the anthologies of critical articles edited by Anderson, Budd, Marks, Simpson, and Smith, among others, as well as in separate sources. The number of books containing interesting chapters on *Huck Finn* is extensive; evaluative summaries of scholarship on *Huck Finn* appear in the annual publication *American Literary Scholarship* (Duke University Press), beginning in 1963. The collections cited below contain the greatest essays on *Huck Finn* up to their publication dates and are thus valuable shortcuts to research in the literature.

Biographies

Anderson, Frederick, et al. *Selected Mark Twain-Howells Letters*. New York: Athenaeum, 1968. A selection of letters from the complete *Mark Twain-Howells Letters* published by the Belknap Press of Harvard University in 1960.

Emerson, Everett. *The Authentic Mark Twain*. Philadelphia: University of Pennsylvania Press, 1984. A recent revisionist biography stressing the repression of Twain's authentic self.

Ferguson, DeLancey. *Mark Twain: Man and Legend*. Indianapolis: Bobbs-Merrill, 1943. The standard critical biography.

Wecter, Dixon. *Sam Clemens of Hannibal*. Boston: Houghton Mifflin, 1952. The best source for the study of characters in Mark Twain's childhood who later appear in *Huck Finn*.

Books

Anderson, Frederic, editor. *Mark Twain the Critical Heritage*. New York: Barnes & Noble, 1971. A collection of critical essays including articles by Brander Matthews, T. S. Perry, and H. L. Mencken.

Beaver, Harold. *Huckleberry Finn*. London: Allen & Unwin, 1987. Good early chapters on composition, reception, and basic analysis.

Blair, Walter. *Mark Twain and Huck Finn*. Berkeley: University of California Press, 1960.

————, editor. *Mark Twain's Hannibal, Huck and Tom*. Berkeley: University of California Press, 1969. Contains the most important background sources for *Huck Finn* from Mark Twain's manuscripts.

Boorstin, Daniel J. *The Americans*. 3 vols. New York: Vintage Press, 1958–1974. An overview of the American spirit that provides a theoretical background documented through American culture and history.

Brooks, Van Wyck. *The Ordeal of Mark Twain*. New York: E. P. Dutton & Co., 1920.

Budd, Louis. *Our Mark Twain: The Making of His Public Personality*. Philadelphia: University of Pennsylvania Press, 1983.

————, editor. *Critical Essays on Mark Twain, 1867–1910*. Boston: G. K. Hall & Co., 1982. A wide-ranging collection of contemporary essays on Twain and his position as humorist and author; a second volume comes forward from 1910.

Burke, Kenneth. *Counter-statement*. Berkeley: University of California Press, 1968.

Clemens, Clara. *My Father Mark Twain*. New York: Harper & Brothers, 1931.

Costanzo, Angelo, editor. *Proteus*, special *Huck Finn* issue, 1:2 (Fall 1984): ix–xi, 1–61. One of the nine articles provides an excellent overview of the first edition, including the altered illustration.

Cox, James M. *Mark Twain the Fate of Humor*. Princeton: Princeton University Press, 1966. Long recognized as one of the most thoughtful studies of the implications of Twain's humor.

Davis, Thadious M., editor. *Black Writers on "Adventures of Huckleberry Finn," One Hundred Years Later*. Mark Twain Journal special issue, 22:2 (Fall 1984): 1–52; a followup book or later issue is projected.

DeVoto, Bernard. *Mark Twain at Work*, Cambridge, Mass.: Harvard University Press, 1942; reprinted, Boston: Houghton Mifflin Sentry, 1968.

————. *Mark Twain's America*. Boston: Little, Brown & Co., 1932; reprinted, Boston: Houghton Mifflin Sentry, 1968.

Howells, W. D. *My Mark Twain*. Baton Rouge: Louisiana State University Press, 1967 (1910). A collection of reviews and a longer personal statement by Twain's most important literary colleague.

Bibliography

Liljegren, S. B. *The Revolt against Romanticism in American Literature as Evidenced in the Works of S. L. Clemens.* New York: Haskell House, 1970 (1945).

Marks, Barry A., editor. *Mark Twain's Huckleberry Finn.* Boston: D. C. Heath and Co., 1959. The primary essays on *Huck Finn* as the great American novel, including essays by Van Wyck Brooks, Walter Blair, Bernard DeVoto, Lionel Trilling, Leo Marx, James Cox, Frank Baldanza, Richard Adams, Lauriat Lane, and William Van O'Connor.

Masters, Edgar Lee. *Mark Twain: A Portrait.* New York: Charles Scribner's Sons, 1938; reprinted, New York: Biblo & Tannan, 1966.

Osterweis, Rollin. *The Myth of the Lost Cause 1865–1900.* Hamden, Conn.: Archon Books, 1973.

Poirier, Richard. *A World Elsewhere: The Place of Style in American Literature.* New York: Oxford University Press, 1966.

Rogers, Franklin R. *Mark Twain's Burlesque Patterns as Seen in the Novels and Narratives, 1855–1885.* Dallas: Southern Methodist University Press, 1960.

Sattelmeyer, Robert, and J. Donald Crowley. *One Hundred Years of Huckleberry Finn.* Columbia: University of Missouri Press, 1985. A centennial collection of essays, several of which have been referred to in this text.

Simpson, Claude M. *Twentieth Century Interpretations of "Adventures of Huckleberry Finn."* Englewood Cliffs, N.J.: Prentice Hall, 1968. A collection of essays including articles by Gladys Bellamy, H. N. Smith, and some major later fiction writers.

Sloane, David E. E. *Mark Twain as Literary Comedian.* Baton Rouge: Louisiana State University Press, 1979. Argues the case for Twain as an egalitarian literary comedian in contradistinction to the prevailing view of his humor as originating in the old Southwest.

Smith, Henry Nash. *Mark Twain: The Development of a Writer.* Cambridge: Harvard University Press, 1962. Generally recognized as the major work on Twain's writing by the dean of modern Twain scholars; includes his discussion of Huck's sound heart and deformed conscience, often anthologized.

———, editor. *Mark Twain: A Collection of Critical Essays.* Englewood Cliffs, N.J.: Prentice-Hall, Inc., 1963. Thirteen essays of which about half deal directly with *Huck Finn*.

Strong, Leah A. *Joseph Hopkins Twichell.* Athens: University of Georgia Press, 1966. Excellent treatment of influence of Hartford Congregational Protestantism on Twain.

Articles

Barchilon, Jose, and Joel Kovel. "*Huckleberry Finn:* A Psychoanalytic Study," *Journal of the American Psychoanalytic Association,* 14 (1966): 775–

814. A valuable interpretation using the tools of psychoanalysis to gain insight into the hero.

Budd, Louis J. "Mark Twain," in *American Literary Scholarship: An Annual* (Durham: Duke University Press, annual). John C. Gerber, Hamlin Hill, and Professor Budd have written the annual analytic bibliography of Twain studies in this volume from 1963 to the present.

Farrell, James T. "Mark Twain's *Huckleberry Finn* and *Tom Sawyer*," in *The League of Frightened Philistines*. New York: Vanguard Press, 1945, pp. 25–30.

Fiedler, Leslie. "Come Back to the Raft Ag'in, Huck Honey!", *Partisan Review*, 15 (June 1948): 664-71. Fiedler examines homosexual tendencies in the novel.

Fischer, Victor. "Huck Finn Reviewed: The Reception of *Huckleberry Finn* in the United States, 1885–1897," *American Literary Realism, 1870–1910*, 16 (Spring 1983): 1–57.

Gribben, Alan. "'I Did Wish Tom Sawyer Was There': Boy-Book Elements in *Tom Sawyer* and *Huckleberry Finn*," in *One Hundred Years of Huckleberry Finn*, pp. 149–70, cited above.

Samossaud, Clara Clemens. "A Personal Remembrance: Tom, Huck, and My Father, Mark Twain," in *The Adventures of Tom Sawyer and the Adventures of Huckleberry Finn*. New York: The Platt & Munk Co., 1960, 9–15.

Scott, Arthur L. "The *Century Magazine* Edits *Huckleberry Finn*, 1884–1885." *American Literature*, 27 (November 1955): 356–62.

Trilling, Lionel. Introduction to *Adventures of Huckleberry Finn* by Mark Twain, New York: Holt, Rinehart & Winston, 1948.

Vogelback, Arthur L. "The Publication and Reception of *Huckleberry Finn* in America." *American Literature*, 11 (November 1939): 260–72.

Historical Sources

Beecher, Catherine E., and Beecher Stowe, Harriet. *The American Woman's Home*. Hartford, Conn.: The Stowe-Day Foundation, 1985 (1869).

Beecher, Henry Ward. "City Boys in the Country," in *Eyes and Ears*. Boston: Ticknor and Fields, 1862.

Brown, Everit, and Strauss, Albert. *A Dictionary of American Politics*. New York: A. L. Burt, 1892 (1882).

Campbell, Helen. *Darkness and Daylight; or, Lights and Shadows of New York Life*. Hartford, Conn.: A. D. Worthington & Co., 1892.

Haines, T. L. and L. W. Yaggy. *The Royal Path of Life*. Springfield, Mass.: W. C. King & Co., 1881 (1876).

Bibliography

Harris, George Washington. *Sut Lovingood's Yarns*. New Haven, Conn.: College and University Press, 1966 (1867).

Hooper, Johnson Jones. *Some Adventures of Captain Simon Suggs, Late of the Tallapoosa Volunteers*. Philadelphia: Carey and Hart, 1845.

Logan, Olive. *The Mimic World*. Philadelphia: New-World Publishing Co., 1871.

Needham, Geo. C. *Street Arabs and Gutter Snipes*. Philadelphia: Hubbard Bros., 1888.

Quod, M. (Charles B. Lewis). "Beyond the Picket Lines; Or, The Army Reminiscence of Captain Jack," *Ballou's Monthly Magazine* 39 (March 1874), 260–71.

Trowbridge, J. T. *Cudjo's Cave*. Boston: J. E. Tilton and Co., 1864.

———. *A Picture of the Desolated States; and the Work of Restoration, 1865–1868*. Hartford: L. Stebbins, 1868.

———. *Young Joe and Other Boys*. Boston: Lee and Shepard, 1879.

Ward, Artemus (Charles F. Browne). *The Complete Works of Artemus Ward*. London: Chatto & Windus, 1922 (1869).

Index

Index

Index

Index

Index

About the Author

David E. E. Sloane is professor of English and director of the Master of Arts in Humanities program at the University of New Haven, Connecticut. A specialist in nineteenth-century American humor, Professor Sloane earned his Ph.D. from Duke University in 1970. His books include *Mark Twain as a Literary Comedian* (Louisiana State Univer-
sit   *east, 1830–*
18   *an Humor*
M   ').